BEST
BAKING

BEST BAKING

THE ESSENTIAL BAKING
BIBLE FOR EVERY COOK

This edition published by Parragon Books Ltd in 2016
LOVE FOOD is an imprint of Parragon Books Ltd

Parragon Books Ltd
Chartist House
15–17 Trim Street
Bath, BA1 1HA, UK
www.parragon.com/lovefood

ISBN: 978-1-4748-5398-9

Printed in China

Notes for the Reader
This book uses both metric and imperial measurements. Follow the same units of measurement throughout; do not mix metric and imperial. All spoon measurements are level: teaspoons are assumed to be 5 ml, and tablespoons are assumed to be 15 ml. Unless otherwise stated, milk is assumed to be full fat, eggs and individual fruits and vegetables are medium, pepper is freshly ground black pepper and salt is table salt. A pinch of salt is calculated as 1/16 of a teaspoon. Unless otherwise stated, all root vegetables should be peeled prior to using.

The times given are an approximate guide only. Preparation times differ according to the techniques used by different people and the cooking times may also vary from those given.

Picture acknowledgements
The publisher would like to thank Getty Images for permission to reproduce copyright material on the following pages: 2, 5, 6–7, 8–9, 10–11, 15, 25, 26, 32–33, 70–71, 108–109, 146–147 and 184–185.

Cover images courtesy of iStock

CONTENTS

Introduction   8

Equipment   10
Ingredients   12
Greasing and Lining Pans   14
Essential Recipes: Cakes   16
Essential Recipes: Pastry   18
Essential Recipes: Biscuits & Cookies   24
Essential Recipes: Breads & Yeast   26
Top Tips for Successful Baking   30
Glossary of Baking Terms   31

Chapter 1: Cakes   32

Victoria Sponge Cake   35
Orange & Poppy Seed Bundt Cake   36
Double Chocolate Mint Sponge   39
Chocolate Fudge Cake   40
Coconut & Lime Cake   43
Clementine Cake   44
Classic Cherry Cake   47
Spiced Apple & Sultana Cake   48
Gingerbread   50
Sticky Toffee Pudding   51
Polenta & Almond Cake   53
Stollen   54
Chocolate & Almond Layer Cake   57
Classic Carrot Cake   58
Banana Loaf   61
Butternut Squash & Orange Cake   62
Lemon Drizzle Cake   65

Double Chocolate Gateaux   66
White Chocolate Coffee Gateaux   69

Chapter 2: Small Cakes & Bars   70

Vanilla Macaroons   73
Hazelnut Chocolate Macaroons   74
Double Chocolate Muffins   77
Warm Spiced Apple Pie Cupcakes   78
Vanilla Frosted Cupcakes   81
Chocolate Chip Brownies   82
Rocky Road Brownies   85
Lamington Cakes   86
Malted Chocolate Bars   88
Macadamia Nut Caramel Squares   89
Chocolate Caramel Shortbread   91
Almond Biscotti   92
Nutty Flapjacks   95
Chocolate Peanut Butter Squares   96
White Chocolate & Apricot Squares   99
Viennese Jam Shortcakes   100
Chocolate Whoopie Pies   103
Hazelnut Bars   104
Date, Pistachio & Honey Slices   107

Chapter 3: Cookies & Biscuits   108

Chocolate Chip Cookies   111
Classic Oatmeal Cookies   112
Peanut Butter Biscuits   115
Almond Cookies with a Cherry on Top   116

Chocolate Chip & Cinnamon Cookies 119
Frosted Orange Biscuits 120
Chocolate Spread & Hazelnut Drops 123
Pecan & Maple Biscuits 124
Banana & Raisin Cookies 126
Coconut & Cranberry Cookies 127
Chunky Apricot & Pecan Cookies 129
Gingersnaps 130
Florentine Biscuits 133
Spiced Rum Biscuits 134
Oaty Raisin & Hazelnut Biscuits 137
Crunchy Muesli Cookies 138
Lemon Chocolate Pinwheels 141
Chocolate & Orange Sandwich Biscuits 142
Crunchy Nut & Honey Sandwich Biscuits 145

Chapter 4: Sweet Pies & Pastries 146

Lemon Meringue Pie 149
Apple Pie 150
Sweet Pumpkin Pie 153
Mississippi Mud Pie 154
Latticed Cherry Pie 157
Pecan Pie 158
Cranberry & Almond Tart 161
Tarte au Citron 162
Ricotta Tart with Chocolate & Walnut 164
Coconut Tart 165
Pear Tart with Chocolate Sauce 167
Plum Crumble Tart 168
Lemon & Passion Fruit Tart 171

Pear & Pecan Strudel 172
Tart Tatin 175
Cream Palmiers 176
Chocolate Parfait Sandwiches 179
One Roll Fruit Pie 180
New York Cheesecake 183

Chapter 5: Bread & Savoury 184

Crusty White Bread 187
Wholemeal Harvest Bread 188
Chilli-Coriander Naan 191
Tomato & Rosemary Focaccia 192
Herb Focaccia 195
Flatbread with Onion & Rosemary 196
Irish Soda Bread 199
Bagels 200
English Muffins 201
Cheese & Chive Bread 203
Olive & Sun-dried Tomato Bread 204
Brioche Plait 207
Tomato & Basil Muffins 208
Chilli Cornbread Muffins 211
Walnut & Pecorino Scones 212
Cheese & Mustard Scones 215
Asparagus & Goat's Cheese Tart 216
Bacon, Onion & Parmesan Tart 219
Potato & Red Onion Pie 220

Index 222

Introduction

Equipment

Oven

A reliable oven is essential to successful baking, and it's a good idea to check yours regularly with an oven thermometer to make sure it's accurate. Preheat the oven to the required temperature for 10–15 minutes before use, so that it has time to reach the correct temperature. Fan ovens cook more quickly than conventional ovens, so cooking times can be reduced by 5–10 minutes per hour, or the temperature can be reduced by 10–20°C/50–68°F.

Resist the temptation to keep opening the oven door to check on your cake, particularly early in the cooking time, as a sudden rush of cold air may cause the cake to sink.

Scales

Many expert cooks can measure ingredients without scales, but for most of us an accurate pair of kitchen scales is essential, particularly for baking. Digital, spring or balance scales are all efficient if used correctly, and most have dual metric and imperial markings or weights. Always follow the same units of measurement throughout – never mix metric and imperial. Make sure your scales are positioned on a level surface, and weigh out all the ingredients before starting to mix.

Measuring Jugs

A heatproof glass or transparent plastic jug is a good choice as it's hard-wearing and easy to clean. Metal and ceramic ones are useful but, being opaque, are less easy to use. Choose one with a good pouring lip and clear markings,

either metric or imperial. Place the jug on a flat surface at eye level for accurate measuring of liquid ingredients.

Measuring Spoons

It's important to use standard measuring spoons, measured level unless stated otherwise, as ordinary kitchen tablespoons and teaspoons can vary in size. Use the blade of a knife, pulled across the spoon, to level off dry ingredients.

Electric Mixer/Food Processor

A hand-held electric mixer with a powerful motor can be used for creaming, whisking, blending and kneading. Table-top mixers, with greater capacity and more power, are useful for all mixtures, particularly large quantities. Food processors can cream, blend or knead, as well as doing other cooking tasks. Again, choose one with a powerful motor for durability. Take care when using a food processor or powerful electric mixer for making cakes as they mix the ingredients very quickly. It is important not to overbeat cake mixtures as this will make them close-textured. Food processors are unsuitable for mixing meringues because the enclosed bowl does not hold enough air to give them volume.

Spoons

Wooden spoons are useful for creaming and mixing. Make sure to keep separate those used for cooking strongly flavoured food, such as onions, as wood can absorb flavours and may transfer them to more delicate mixtures. Heat-

resistant nylon or melamine spoons are durable and less flavour-absorbent. A large metal spoon is useful for folding in ingredients.

Spatula

You'll find a flexible rubber or silicone spatula helpful for light mixing and for scraping out bowls cleanly. Some have a spoon-shaped blade which helps when transferring cake mix from the bowl to the tin.

Bowls

A selection of different-sized mixing bowls is essential, and a set of toughened glass bowls is a good basic start as they are durable, heatproof and easy to clean. Melamine, polythene and ceramic bowls often have pouring lips, and some have non-slip bases to grip the worktop.

Wire Cooling Racks

A wire rack allows your cakes to cool evenly and prevents condensation, which can cause soggy texture and poor keeping quality. They vary from a simple metal rectangle, to expanding three-tier ones, which are useful for large batches of baking. Some have a non-stick coating for easier cleaning.

Sieve

A good-quality, rustproof metal or nylon sieve is necessary for sifting together dry ingredients evenly, and a set of three sizes is useful. Nylon ones are hard-wearing and will withstand boiling water, but metal ones are the most durable and will last for years.

Graters

A hard-wearing, stainless steel box grater, or flat 'Microplane' type graters with firm grip handles, are good for grating citrus rind, cheese, apple, chocolate, nutmeg, etc. You'll need a fine, medium and coarse grater. Some also have a slicing option.

Citrus Squeezer/Reamer

A sturdy plastic, metal, toughened glass or ceramic squeezer is used for extracting juice from citrus fruits. For smooth juice you'll need one with a filter to extract all the fibres from the juice. A wooden or plastic reamer squeezes out the juice by simply pushing into the halved fruit, but you may also get some pips.

Rolling Pin

For rolling pastry and biscuit doughs, a wooden rolling pin is a good tool and you can shape and cool tuiles on it too.

Marble, granite or glass rolling pins are more expensive but their cool, smooth surface is good for rolling sticky mixtures.

Pastry Brush

A pastry brush is the easiest way to grease cake tins evenly, and can also be used for applying glazes. They are available with natural bristles or more durable synthetic bristles. Do make sure you clean brushes thoroughly after use.

Cookie Cutters

A set of round cookie cutters, with either plain or fluted edges, is a good basic choice, preferably in metal. Later you can add fancy-shaped cutters. Make sure the cutting edge is sharp and the top edge is rolled to protect your fingers and keep the cutter rigid.

Piping Bag and Nozzles

For decorative piping of icing, frostings or soft mixtures, you'll need piping bags and nozzles. Strong nylon or fabric bags are washable and re-usable, while disposable bags save work. A small selection of stainless steel nozzles should include a plain writing, small and large star and plain large nozzles.

Ingredients

Flour

Wheat flour is the most commonly used flour for baking. The amount of gluten (protein) in wheat flour varies between the different types.

Plain white flour has the bran and wheat germ removed, and is then fortified with vitamins. Soft plain flour is made from wheat with a low gluten content. It has a fine texture and is ideal for making cakes, pastry and biscuits. Strong plain flour is milled from wheat with a high gluten content and is used for breads and in most yeast baking.

Self-raising flour is plain white flour with baking powder added as a raising agent. To make your own self-raising flour add 2 teaspoons of baking powder to each 225 g/8 oz plain flour.

Wholemeal flour is flour that has been milled from the whole wheat grain. It is coarser and heavier than white flour. It is available as a strong (high-gluten) flour for breadmaking and a soft (lower-gluten) flour for cakes and pastry.

Other flours such as brown flour, malted flour, cornflour, buckwheat, rye, rice and chestnut flours are also sometimes used in baking. Each has its own unique characteristic or flavour.

Sugars

Most sugar is produced from one of two sources: sugar cane or sugar beet. There are a number of different types of sugar, each with its own particular qualities. Unrefined sugars are made from sugar cane and have a higher mineral, vitamin and trace element content than refined sugars.

Granulated sugar can be used to achieve a crunchy texture in some biscuits and in cakes prepared by the rubbing-in method (see page 16).

Caster sugar has a finer crystal and dissolves more readily. This is the type used most frequently in baking. It is known as caster sugar because it can be placed in a caster – a container with a perforated top, similar to a flour dredger.

Golden granulated, golden caster and golden icing sugar are the unrefined forms of the refined sugars.

Molasses sugar is a dark, fine-grained unrefined sugar with a strong flavour, used when baking rich fruit cakes.

Dark muscovado sugar is an unrefined sugar that has a less intense flavour than molasses sugar, but a good, dark colour. It is ideal for light fruit cakes and gingerbread.

Light muscovado sugar is lighter in colour and flavour than the dark variety and is used widely in cakes, muffins, teabreads, biscuits and cookies.

Demerara sugar is a large, coarse-grained brown sugar that can be made

from either refined or unrefined sugar. As well as being used in baking, it is sometimes sprinkled over the tops of pies, crumbles and cakes for its crunchy texture.

Soft light and dark brown sugars are similar to light and dark muscovado sugars. They are usually refined white sugar that has been tossed in molasses or syrup.

Icing sugar is very fine and powdery and dissolves almost instantly. It is used in some biscuits and pastry, and for making icing, frosting and fillings.

Fats

Butter produces the best flavour. Unsalted butter is generally considered best for baking. If you use salted butter, you will not need to add any extra salt to the recipe (except for breadmaking). Use butter straight from the refrigerator for pastry making and at room temperature for cake making.

Margarine is preferred over butter by some people for baking. Block margarine is generally the best, but soft tub margarine is needed for making cakes by the all-in-one method (see page 16).

Low-fat spreads are not suitable for baking, as they contain a high proportion of water.

Suet made from either shredded beef fat or solidified vegetable oils is used for making suet crust pastry.

Lard and white vegetable fat have a bland flavour, but give a light, short texture to pastry and biscuits, so are sometimes used. They are usually combined with butter for flavour.

Eggs

The size of eggs used in baking is important. Store eggs in the refrigerator away from strong-smelling foods. Remove from the refrigerator to return to room temperature before using if possible, as cold eggs do not combine as well with other ingredients or trap as much air.

Raising Agents

Baking powder is a mixture of cream of tartar and bicarbonate of soda. When mixed with moisture, it releases carbon dioxide, a harmless gas that expands during baking to make the food rise.

Bicarbonate of soda produces carbon dioxide when mixed with an acid such as lemon juice or buttermilk. This reaction means that it can be used as a raising agent.

Yeast is a single-cell organism that converts the natural sugars in flour to produce carbon dioxide. Yeast needs warmth, moisture and food (sugars) to work. It is available in both dried and fresh forms for baking.

Greasing and Lining Pans

Not all cake tins need to be fully lined for baking. For many simple sponges you just need to give the base and sides of the tin a quick brush of oil or melted butter and insert a piece of non-stick baking paper in the base. Richer or low-fat mixtures usually need a thoroughly greased and lined tin to prevent sticking.

Lining a round tin

1 Grease the tin. Cut a strip of baking paper about 2.5 cm/1 inch longer than the circumference and about 2.5 cm/1 inch deeper than the tin.

2 Fold up one long edge about 1 cm/½ inch, then unfold, leaving a crease.

3 Use scissors to snip cuts along the folded edge of the paper, so that it can be eased into the tin to fit around the curve at the base.

4 Place the tin on a sheet of baking paper and draw around it with a pencil to mark the size. Cut with scissors just inside the line, making a round to fit inside the base, covering the snipped edges of the side lining paper. Grease the paper.

Lining a square tin

1 Grease the tin. Cut a strip of baking paper about 2.5 cm/1 inch longer than the circumference of the tin and 2.5 cm/1 inch deeper.

2 Fold up one long edge about 1 cm/½ inch, then unfold, leaving a crease. Fit the paper into the sides of the tin, cutting a diagonal slit into the folded edge to fit each corner.

3 Place the tin on a sheet of baking paper, draw around it to mark the size, then cut just inside the line to make a square. Lay the square inside the tin, covering the folded edges. Grease the paper.

Lining a Swiss roll tin or traybake tin

1 Grease the base and sides of the tin. Cut a piece of baking paper 7 cm/2¾ inches larger than the tin.

2 Place the tin on the paper, then make a cut from each corner of the paper in towards the tin corner.

3 Place the paper inside the tin so that the diagonally cut corners overlap and fit neatly. Grease the paper.

Lining a loaf tin

1 Grease the tin. Cut a strip of baking paper the length of the base and wide enough to cover the base and long sides. Place in the tin.

2 Cut a second piece of baking paper the width of the tin base and long enough to cover the base and ends of the tin. Slot this in over the first piece to line the tin, then grease the paper.

Lining and flouring a tin

1 Grease the base and sides of the tin, then slip a piece of non-stick baking paper in the base. Grease the paper.

2 Sprinkle a little flour into the tin. Tilt the tin, tapping lightly, so the flour coats the base and sides evenly. Tip out any excess.

Essential Recipes: Cakes

The main ingredients for making cakes are flour, fat, sugar and eggs. The proportion of fat to flour will influence the method by which the cake is made. With half or less fat to flour, the rubbing-in method is used, while with half or more fat to flour, the creaming method is used. If little or no fat is used, then whisking is the appropriate method.

Creamed Cakes

The most well-known of cakes made by this method is the Victoria Sponge Cake, which uses butter, sugar, eggs and flour in equal quantities to make a light and airy cake. It makes a good base for many variations. Cakes made by this method should have a light, even texture. The higher the proportion of fat, sugar and eggs to flour, the richer the cake will be.

Storage Cakes made by the creaming method keep well in an airtight tin. Undecorated cakes freeze well.

All-in-One Cakes

This is a simplified variation of the creaming method. All the ingredients are beaten together at once until smooth. Extra baking powder helps to make the cake rise and soft margarine or butter is essential for it to mix fully.

This gives a close-textured cake and is an ideal method when you are short of time.

Whisked Sponge Cakes

These can be made with or without any fat. Whisked sponges depend on the amount of air trapped in the eggs and sugar during the whisking of the eggs. The bowl should be warmed and the eggs at room temperature. The best results are achieved using an electric whisk. Care has to be taken not to knock the air out when folding in the flour, which must be done with a lightness of hand.

Storage Fat-free sponges are best eaten on the day they are made. Those with some fat will keep a little longer if stored in an airtight container.

Rubbed-in Cakes

This method of cake mixing produces a plain, coarse texture and is most often used for teabreads, scones and buns. The proportion of fat to flour varies from 25 per cent to around 66 per cent. Rubbing in the fat with the fingertips held high over the bowl incorporates air. Liquid is added and the mixture is then gently brought together. Be careful not to overwork the mixture or the results will be tough. Baking powder is usually added to assist the raising.

Storage Rubbed-in cakes should be kept for no more than three days, as they tend to become dry over time.

Creamed Cakes

All-in-One Cakes

Whisked Sponge Cakes

Melted cakes

A few dense, moist cakes such as gingerbread employ this method. The fat and sugar are melted together before the dry ingredients are stirred in.

Storage These cakes are best left for one day before eating. They keep well in an airtight container.

Small Cakes

The same basic principles and techniques used for making large cakes apply to small cakes. However, for small cakes the oven temperature is usually higher and the cooking time much shorter. Small cakes, not much more than a couple of bites in size, can be cooked in a 12-hole bun tray. For more substantial individual cakes, a muffin tray can be used. Lining the tins with paper cake cases will ensure that they turn out easily. Some small cakes are made as one large cake and then cut into appropriately sized bars or squares. This is a quick way of producing individual cakes.

Curdling in Cake Mixture

Curdling is the term used when the water from the eggs separates out from the fat globules in the cake mixture, and is usually caused by the eggs being too cold. A curdled cake mixture will hold less air and will produce a cake with a dense texture. To help prevent curdling, use eggs at room temperature. If your mixture does begin to curdle, beat in a tablespoon of the measured flour to help bind the mixture back together.

Is it Cooked?

Follow the timings in the recipe as a guideline, but also rely on your own judgement, as ovens vary in temperature. Small cakes should be well risen, firm and springy to the touch, and sponge cakes should be springy to the touch.

Test by gently pressing the cake with a finger. Once you have removed your finger, the cake should spring back, but if you can still see the fingerprint, return the cake to the oven for a further few minutes. Fruit cakes and deep sponge cakes are best tested with a skewer, inserted into the centre. The skewer should come out clean when the cake is cooked. For most cakes, leave to cool for a few minutes in the tin before turning out and transferring to a wire rack to cool completely. Some cakes such as rich fruit cakes benefit from being allowed to cool completely in the tin – the recipe will specify this where necessary.

Rubbed-in Cakes

Melted Cakes

Small Cakes

Essential Recipes: Pastry

Basic pastry is not as difficult to make as is sometimes perceived. Although preparing other, more specialist pastries does require a certain amount of skill, following the recipes closely will enable you to acquire that skill quickly and a little practice will help you to achieve professional results.

Cooking Pastry

The oven must be hot when the pastry is first put in so that it will rise when the air that it contains is heated. The gluten in the flour absorbs the water and stretches and entangles the air in the pastry as the air expands. The heat of the oven then sets the pastry in its risen shape. As it cooks, the starch grains in the flour will also burst and absorb the fat. If the oven is too cool, the fat will melt and run out while the flour remains uncooked, resulting in a heavy, soggy and greasy pastry. After the pastry is set, the temperature can be reduced to cook the filling, if required.

Types of Pastry

All kinds of pastry, except suet crust, use plain flour. Wholemeal flour can be used instead of white, but it produces heavier results and requires extra liquid to bring it together.

Shortcrust Pastry

Perhaps the most common home-baked pastry, this is also one of the easiest to master, as long as the basic rules of pastry making are followed. A proportion of half fat to flour is used.

225 g/8 oz plain flour
115 g/4 oz butter
2–3 tbsp cold water

Basic Method

1 Sift the flour into a bowl.

2 Cut the butter into small cubes and add to the flour. Rub in using your fingertips, lifting your hands high above the bowl to incorporate more air. The mixture will resemble fine breadcrumbs when the butter has been fully rubbed in.

3 Stir in any additional flavourings, if using, such as ground nuts or cheese, or sugar for sweet pastry.

4 Add the water gradually and use your fingers to bring the pastry together. Turn out the dough onto a lightly floured work surface and knead very lightly. Ideally, the pastry should be wrapped in foil or clingfilm and chilled in the refrigerator for 30 minutes to allow the pastry to 'relax', which helps to prevent it shrinking when it is baked.

5 Roll out the dough on a lightly floured work surface. Rolling should be carried out in short, sharp strokes, with a light, even pressure in a forward movement only. Turn the pastry as you roll.

6 Use as required, then allow the pastry to relax again in a cool place for 15–30 minutes before baking. This is especially important if you have not previously relaxed the pastry.

7 Bake in a hot oven for 15–20 minutes until set. The temperature may then be reduced.

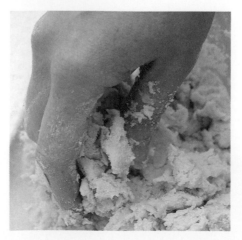

Baking Blind

When used to line a tin, shortcrust pastry is often precooked to set the pastry before the filling is added. The term used to describe this is 'baking blind'.

1 Line the tin with the rolled-out pastry and prick the base with a fork.

2 Chill for about 30 minutes in the refrigerator or 10 minutes in the freezer (you can also bake pastry cases blind from frozen).

3 Line the pastry case with a sheet of non-stick baking paper, greaseproof paper or foil and fill with purpose-made ceramic or metal baking beans or dried pulses or rice. These baking beans help to conduct heat and cook the pastry, as well as preventing the pastry puffing up in the centre.

4 Bake for 10 minutes, then remove the paper and beans and bake for a further 10 minutes until the pastry is just golden.

5 Remove from the oven and brush a little beaten egg or egg white over the base to seal (the heat of the pastry will cook the egg).

Cook's Tip

It is important to follow a few basic rules when making pastry. Always measure the ingredients accurately and keep everything cool. Always use a light touch and handle the pastry with care. Knead the dough just sufficiently to bind it together – over-kneading will start to develop the gluten in the flour and result in a tough, greasy pastry. Roll out pastry lightly, taking care not to stretch it unduly. Use only a small amount of flour when rolling out to avoid upsetting the careful balance of ingredients. Allow the pastry to rest in the refrigerator, wrapped in foil or clingfilm, before rolling. A little salt may be added to bring out the flavour of pastry, but if salted butter or margarine is used, this is usually unnecessary.

Puff Pastry

Both flaky and puff pastry are more difficult and very time consuming to prepare, but their richness, especially in the case of puff pastry, gives them a superior flavour. Puff pastry has the highest proportion of fat to flour and is therefore the most difficult to handle. The principle behind the pastry is to create many layers of dough and butter by folding and turning the two together.

350 g/12 oz plain flour
175 g/6 oz butter
8 tbsp cold water

Basic Method

1 Sift the flour into a bowl and rub in a quarter of the butter.

2 Add the water and use your fingers to bring the pastry together. Knead briefly to form a smooth dough. Put in a polythene bag and chill in the refrigerator for 30 minutes.

3 Roll out the remaining butter between two sheets of clingfilm to form a block about 1 cm/½ inch thick.

4 Roll out the dough to a square about four times the size of the block of butter.

5 Put the block of butter in the centre of the dough and fold over the corners of the dough to completely enclose the butter.

6 Roll out the dough into a rectangle three times as long as it is wide.

7 Fold one third of the dough over to cover the middle third, then fold the remainder over the top.

8 Give the dough a half turn, roll out to form another rectangle and fold again as before. Repeat the initial rolling and folding six times in total, chilling the dough frequently between rolling.

9 Leave to relax for a final 30 minutes, then use as required. Trim the folded edges of the pastry before using to assist the rising. Bake in a hot oven. The pastry should rise to 6–8 times its original height.

Flaky Pastry

This uses a slightly lower proportion of fat to flour – two thirds to three quarters fat to flour – and the fat is added in stages. It is advisable to use a strong plain flour for flaky pastry. After the initial fat has been added, the dough is kneaded to develop the elasticity of the gluten, resulting in an elastic dough that will rise easily. The pastry must be allowed to relax before being baked.

225 g/8 oz plain flour
175 g/6 oz butter
6–7 tbsp cold milk or water

Basic Method

1 Sift the flour into a bowl and rub in a quarter of the butter.

2 Add the milk and use your fingers to bring the pastry together. Knead briefly to form a smooth dough.

3 Roll out the dough into a rectangle three times as long as it is wide.

4 Dot one third of the remaining butter over two thirds of the pastry in rough lumps. Fold the uncovered dough over to cover half the buttered dough, then fold the remaining third over the top.

5 Seal the edges of the dough by pressing down with a rolling pin.

6 Give the dough a half turn, roll out to form another rectangle and repeat steps 4 and 5 twice more until all the butter has been used. Put the pastry in a polythene bag and chill in the refrigerator for 30 minutes.

7 Roll and fold the pastry three more times, as before, but without the addition of butter. Leave to relax for a final 30 minutes, then use as required. Trim the folded edges of the pastry before using to assist the rising. Bake in a hot oven.

Rough Puff Pastry

This pastry is relatively easy to make and produces a fabulous light, flaky pastry. It can be a little sticky to handle to begin with. It has a similar fat content to flaky pastry.

225 g/8 oz plain flour
175 g/6 oz butter
6–7 tbsp cold milk or water

Basic Method

1 Sift the flour into a bowl. Cut the butter into 2.5-cm/1-inch dice and add to the flour.

2 Add the milk and use your fingers to bring the pastry together. Knead very lightly.

3 Roll and fold the pastry as for puff pastry. Chill for 30 minutes before using and bake in a hot oven.

Suet Crust Pastry

Suet crust pastry is a filling, homely kind of pastry. Self-raising flour (or plain flour and baking powder) is used to make this.

225 g/8 oz plain flour
115 g/4 oz suet
2 tsp baking powder
150 ml/5 fl oz cold water

Basic Method

1 Sift the flour into a bowl.

2 Stir in the suet and baking powder.

3 Add enough water to form an elastic dough.

4 Roll out the dough only once, to avoid producing a hard pastry.

Hot Water Crust Pastry

This traditional type of pastry is used for raised pies, such as pork or game pies. It is the exception to one of the basic rules of pastry making in that its success depends on the warmth of the utensils and flour throughout the making and shaping. If it becomes too cold, it will be difficult to handle.

225 g/8 oz plain flour
85 g/3 oz lard
5 tbsp water

Basic Method

1 Sift the flour into a bowl and make a well in the centre.

2 Put the lard and water in a saucepan and heat until the lard melts, then bring to the boil. Immediately add to the well in the flour, mix with a spoon to form a dough, then knead the dough.

3 The pastry should be shaped while still warm and cooked in a hot oven.

Choux Pastry

This rich, soft pastry relies on its high water content, which becomes very hot during cooking, to form a hollow pastry shell.

85 g/3 oz strong plain flour
55 g/2 oz butter
150 ml/5 fl oz water
2 eggs

Basic Method

1 Sift the flour into a bowl.

2 Put the butter and water in a saucepan and heat until the butter has melted.

3 Add the flour to the saucepan all at once and beat with a wooden spoon until the mixture forms a ball around the spoon. Leave to cool slightly.

4 Gradually beat in the eggs until the dough is smooth and glossy. The more the mixture is beaten, the better the results, as more air will be incorporated.

5 Shape by piping or with a spoon, as required. Bake in a hot oven.

Covering a Pie

This is the basic method for making a single crust to cover a savoury or sweet pie filling. You can then add decorative details and a glaze to enhance the appearance of the pie.

1 Roll out the pastry to about 5 cm/2 inches larger all round than the top of the dish.

2 Cut a strip about 2.5 cm/1 inch wide from the edge of the pastry.

3 Moisten the edge of the dish and stick the pastry strip to the dish.

4 Fill the pie and dampen the pastry strip with a little water.

5 Using a rolling pin, carefully lift the pastry over the pie. Press the edge down to seal.

6 Using a sharp knife, trim the edge and make a small hole in the centre of the pie to allow the steam to escape.

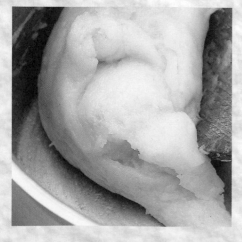

Pastry Finishes

Use a blunt knife to tap the edge of the pie and knock it up. This also helps to seal the pie fully.

Press the edge with a floured fork.

Press one thumb around the edge of the pie while pinching the outside edge between your other thumb and forefinger.

Press a thumb around the edge and draw a knife in a short distance from the edge towards the centre of the pie between each thumbprint to create a scalloped edge.

Decorate the pie by using the pastry trimmings. Cut them into leaves or other shapes, as desired, and stick to the pastry crust by moistening them slightly.

Glazes

Glazing the pastry will produce a shiny golden surface once baked. You can use milk, beaten egg mixed with a little water, or lightly beaten egg white. Brush a thin layer over the pastry with a pastry brush, but avoid making the pastry too wet. For sweet pies, a little caster sugar can be sprinkled on top.

Essential Recipes: Biscuits & Cookies

In recent times the name 'cookie' has been widely adopted along with the spread in popularity of the traditionally American-style chunky variety, such as the chocolate chip cookie. You can find a biscuit or cookie that is perfect for any occasion, be it a decadent coffee morning, a hearty afternoon tea, an elegant dinner or a packed lunch on the run.

Because biscuits bake quickly, you will need to keep a close eye on the baking until you become more experienced in gauging the exact cooking time easily. For most biscuits, leave to cool on the baking sheet for a few minutes before transferring to a wire rack to cool completely. Many biscuits are very soft when they come out of the oven but crisp on cooling, so remember to remove them from the tin before they become completely cold or they may stick. Store in an airtight container to retain freshness and crispness. Most biscuits also freeze well – simply thaw at room temperature.

Rolled and Moulded Biscuits

Here the biscuit dough is rolled out and cut out or shaped into logs, balls or crescents. Take care not to add too much extra flour when rolling and shaping, as this will alter the careful balance of the ingredients. If a dough is very soft, you may find it easier to roll out between two sheets of clingfilm. Try to avoid rerolling too many times, or the biscuits may become tough.

Dropped Biscuits

These are the quickest and easiest to make. They are often made by the creaming method, where the fat and sugar are beaten together, then the flour and any additional flavourings such as nuts or chocolate chips are added. The mixture is then beaten just enough to bring all the ingredients together in a soft dough, which can then be dropped onto the baking sheet from spoons. Always place the drops of dough spaced well apart on the baking sheet, as the biscuits will spread during baking.

Piped Biscuits

Some biscuits are piped from a plain or fluted piping nozzle to produce a decorative effect. The consistency of the dough needs to be just right – if it is too stiff it will be hard to pipe; if it is too soft the biscuits will lose their shape when baked.

Wafer-thin Biscuits

Some classic biscuits are very thin and crisp. The mixture is very soft (that of a batter) and is spooned onto a baking sheet and spread out to form a round. These are probably the hardest biscuits to make, as they bake very rapidly. They are sometimes shaped into rolls or curled. In this case, you need to work fast, only baking a couple at a time, as they need to be shaped while still warm.

Sliced Biscuits

The firm dough for these can be shaped into a log and the biscuits are sliced at the desired thickness. The uncooked dough can be stored in the refrigerator for several days and a few biscuits cut from the log and baked as desired. This is an ideal way of making freshly baked biscuits every day.

Essential Recipes: Breads & Yeast

The many different kinds of home-made bread could easily fill a book in themselves. Once you've mastered the basics, such as soda bread, plain white bread, malt bread and rolls, you can move on to making delicious flavoured breads. Sweet yeast breads and buns are delicious for breakfast, high tea or a snack. You will also find a selection of breads made without yeast in this book.

Yeast cookery is not particularly difficult and the results are most rewarding. Unlike when working with pastry, a warm kitchen will help you on the way. Also, there is no need for the caution in handling that pastry requires – a firm hand is perfect for kneading the dough to develop the gluten content of the bread, which gives it its unique texture. Of course, you do need to allow more time to produce yeasted products, but they can usually be left alone to rise and prove while you are free to do other things. Most yeasted breads and bakes freeze well, so they are ideal for batch baking. The frozen bakes can be thawed at room temperature and refreshed in a hot oven for 5 minutes to warm through before serving.

Types of Yeast

Yeast is the raising agent most frequently used for breads. It is a living organism that, when active, creates carbon dioxide. Small bubbles of carbon dioxide then become trapped within the structure of the dough, giving bread its characteristic structure. There are two main types of bread yeasts available: fresh and dried.

Fresh Yeast

This can be purchased from health food shops and some bakeries. It has a creamy colour and is moist and firm. Fresh yeast is usually dissolved in the liquid and allowed a preliminary fermentation before being added to the remaining ingredients. It will keep for only a few days in the refrigerator, but it can be frozen for up to three months.

Dried Yeast

This is available in two forms. Regular dried yeast requires a preliminary fermentation and is activated by mixing with a little liquid and sugar or flour. Easy-blend dried yeast, fast-action dried yeast and instant dried yeast are just different names for yeast that does not require this preliminary fermentation and is simply stirred into the flour before the liquid is added.

The first rising and knocking back can also be eliminated if time is short. Dried yeast has a longer shelf life than fresh yeast and does not need to be refrigerated.

Effects of Temperature on Yeast

Yeast works quickest in warm temperatures, so it is recommended that the dough is left in a warm place to rise. However, yeast does not stop working at lower temperatures – it simply slows down. Therefore, dough can be made, shaped and then left to rise overnight in a refrigerator. Allow the dough to return to room temperature before baking.

Effects of Other Ingredients on Yeast Action

A basic loaf consists of just flour, yeast, salt and water, but some breads as well as buns, cakes and even pastries are made with yeast doughs that have been enriched with other ingredients such as butter, sugar and eggs. Additional ingredients may contribute to the rising, give added colour to the crumb and crust and may also improve the keeping qualities. However, all these additional ingredients will have an effect on the action of yeast.

Sugar in small amounts speeds up the action of yeast, but in larger quantities – above 55 g/2 oz per 450 g/1 lb – it will retard the action of yeast.

Fat in proportions above 25 g/1 oz per 450 g/1 lb will retard the action of yeast.

Eggs have a fat content and may slow the action of yeast, but they can also retain air in the mixture, so often help to produce a lighter texture.

To overcome any adverse effects of these added ingredients:

• Allow additional time for the rising – 2 hours or more is not unusual.
• Make the dough in two parts, adding the additional ingredients after an initial rising.
• Extra yeast may be added.

Gluten

Gluten is formed by a combination of two proteins, gliadin and glutenin, which are found in wheat flour. Strong flours have a higher proportion of these proteins than soft flour. When these proteins are hydrated, they bond with each other, creating a large protein called gluten that gives the bread its structure. The longer the dough is kneaded, the stronger the gluten becomes and the better texture the bread has. It is possible to knead the dough so much that it becomes too warm and the gluten begins to break down, but this is very unlikely to happen if kneading by hand. If you choose to knead in a mixer, knead for short bursts, allowing a few seconds each time for the dough to cool slightly.

Yeast-free Breads

Some breads do not contain yeast. These breads use another method to leaven the bread (make the bread rise) or are unleavened. Sometimes called quick breads, soda bread and corn bread fall into the former category. Bicarbonate of soda or baking powder is added to the dough. These produce carbon dioxide, a process that begins as soon as the dough is mixed, so the bread must be baked immediately. The dough should be soft and sticky, and in some cases is more like a thick batter. Quick breads have a soft, crumbly texture and some are best served warm.

Unleavened breads are sometimes called flat breads. Some flat breads, such as naan and pitta bread are in fact leavened with yeast or baking powder but unleavened dough can also be used. Flat breads are among the oldest breads. Paratha, tortillas and chapattis are all examples of yeast-free flat breads. Flat breads can be topped like pizza and focaccia, stuffed like pitta bread, filled with beans and rice and rolled like chapattis or tortillas, or used for dipping like poppadoms from India.

Making Yeast Breads
Basic method

The method used is basically the same for all yeast breads, although individual steps may vary according to the recipe.

675 g/1 lb 8 oz strong white flour
2 tsp salt
2 tsp easy-blend dried yeast
about 450 ml/16 fl oz lukewarm water
2 tbsp olive oil or 25 g/1 oz butter

1 Sift the flour and salt into a large bowl. Stir in the yeast and make a well in the centre. Pour the liquid into the well and mix until you have a soft, sticky dough.

2 Turn out the dough onto a lightly floured work surface and begin kneading by folding the dough over on top of itself and pushing away with the heel of your hand – do not be afraid to be quite forceful. Keep kneading, giving the dough a quarter turn as you do so, for 10 minutes, or until the dough is very smooth and elastic and no longer sticky. Alternatively, knead the dough in an electric mixer fitted with a dough hook for 6–8 minutes.

3 Form the dough into a ball and put in a lightly oiled bowl. Rub a little oil over the surface of the dough to prevent it drying out and cover loosely with clingfilm or slide the bowl inside a clean

polythene bag. Leave to rise in a warm place for 1 hour, or until doubled in size.

4 When the dough has increased to double its original size, turn out onto a lightly floured work surface and lightly knead again for a few minutes. This is called 'knocking back', as some of the air that has been incorporated into the dough is knocked out and the dough shrinks in size. This ensures that the bread has a more even texture, as any large air pockets are removed at this stage.

5 Shape the dough as required and place in a lightly greased baking tin or on a tray. If placing in a tin, the dough should half-fill the tin.

6 Cover loosely again and leave to rise (prove) for a second time until doubled in size.

7 Bake in a hot oven. To test if the bread is cooked, turn out of the tin and tap the base. The loaf should sound hollow. Leave to cool on a wire rack.

Bread Machines

You can make bread with the minimum of fuss and effort by using a bread machine. Once all the ingredients have been weighed and added to the pan, the machine can be left to do the hard work and a few hours later you have a freshly baked loaf. As most machines have a timer, you can set yours so that you can enjoy freshly baked bread when you wake up in the morning. Always follow the manufacturer's instructions, as quantities of ingredients and methods may vary.

A Note About Salt

Salt is an essential ingredient in breadmaking, as it not only adds flavour but also strengthens the gluten structure, and helps control the growth of yeast. Too little and the result will be a poor gluten structure; too much and the salt will inhibit the action of the yeast. Both will result in a loaf of poor volume and flavour. For this reason, it is important not to vary the amount of salt in a recipe, even if you are trying to reduce your salt intake, as this will adversely affect the finished product.

Top Tips for Successful Baking

Before you Start

• Always preheat the oven to the correct temperature, so it's ready to use when your cake is mixed. Allow at least 10 minutes for preheating.

• Grease tins lightly with a mild-flavoured oil, such as sunflower oil, or melted butter. Use a pastry brush to coat the tin quickly and evenly.

• For creamed mixtures, such as sponge cakes, line the base of the tin with non-stick baking paper; for rich mixtures and fruit cakes, line the base and sides of the tin. For very rich fruit cakes, wrap a double thickness of brown paper around the outside of the tin for extra protection and tie with string to secure.

• If you don't have the correct-sized tin for the recipe, or prefer to use an unusual-shaped tin, just match the capacity – e.g. a 20-cm/8-inch round tin holds about the same volume of liquid as an 18-cm/7-inch square tin.

• Assemble and weigh all your ingredients before you start to mix.

The Perfect Mix

• Always sift the flour with any raising agents or spices before adding to a mixture so that they are evenly distributed.

• If you run out of self-raising flour, add 2 teaspoons of baking powder to each 225 g/8 oz of plain flour and sift together thoroughly before use.

• Most cake recipes use either butter or hard (block) margarine, which are interchangeable, although butter has a much better flavour. Soft (tub) margarines and oil are good for all-in-one recipes, but less successful for creamed methods. Low-fat spreads have a high water content and give poor results in conventional recipes.

• For most recipes, fats should be used at room temperature for ease of mixing. Butter or block margarine can be softened for a few seconds in the microwave to make mixing easier.

• It's best to use eggs at room temperature for baking as they give a better volume and hold more air when whisked. If you usually store your eggs in the refrigerator, remove them about 30 minutes before you start to mix.

• To separate eggs, tap the shell against the side of a mixing bowl to crack, then break open, letting the white run out into the bowl and holding the yolk in one half of the shell. Tip the yolk backwards and forwards from shell to shell to let all the white run into the bowl.

• When folding in flour, use a metal spoon, cutting through the mixture with a light, quick action to keep as much air in it as possible. Over-mixing can result in a heavy, close-textured cake.

Baked to Perfection

• Unless otherwise stated, place your cake on the centre shelf of the oven to bake. With fan ovens, the temperature should be the same throughout the oven, but follow the manufacturer's instructions for specific guidelines.

• Resist the temptation to open the oven door too often during cooking, and close it gently rather than banging it shut. It's best to try to wait until at least halfway through the cooking time before sneaking a look. A quick peep won't harm the cake, but if you open the door too often the temperature will drop and may prevent the cake rising properly.

• To test light sponge cakes for doneness, press the top lightly with a fingertip – the cake should feel spongy to the touch, and should spring back when pressed. To check rich fruit cakes for doneness, listen closely – if the cake is still sizzling inside, it is not yet thoroughly cooked. Most large cakes will shrink slightly from the sides of the tin when they are cooked. As a final test, insert a skewer or thin knife into the centre of the cake, then lift it out. If the cake is cooked it should come out clean; if it's sticky, the mixture needs more cooking.

• Most cakes should be cooled slightly in the tin before turning out. They shrink from the sides of the tin and become firmer, so turning them out is easier.

• Use a wire rack for cooling cakes to ensure that any excess steam can escape without making the cake soggy. If you don't have a wire rack, use the rack from a grill pan or a barbecue rack.

• Always make sure your cake is completely cool before storing, as any remaining steam can cause mould. Store cakes for short periods in a ventilated container such as a tin with a close-fitting lid. Use airtight containers or sealed polythene bags for freezing.

Glossary of Baking Terms

Baking Blind
A method of baking a pastry-lined flan or tart tin without filling. Place a round of baking paper or greaseproof paper on top of the pastry and fill with dried beans, rice or ceramic baking beans, then bake as the recipe instructs.

Beating
A method of vigorously agitating with a spoon, fork or whisk, to combine ingredients evenly, to soften ingredients, such as butter, or to incorporate air into mixtures.

Creaming
The beating together of a mixture of fat and sugar to soften to a pale, fluffy consistency, incorporating air into the mix to make a light, spongy cake, such as a Victoria Sponge Cake.

Dredging
The sprinkling of a mixture or surface generously with a dry ingredient, such as flour or icing sugar, either using a sieve or a 'dredger' pot, which has a top with holes for even sprinkling.

Dusting
The sprinkling of a surface lightly with a dry ingredient, such as flour, icing sugar or spices, to give a thin coating, using a fine sieve or dredger to distribute the ingredient evenly.

Folding In
A method of combining a creamed mixture with dry ingredients, or to incorporate whisked egg whites, so that as little air is knocked out as possible. Ideally, use a large metal spoon to cut and fold the dry ingredients through the mixture, agitating as little as possible to retain air bubbles for lightness.

Glazing
The brushing of a coating over a mixture either before or after baking, to give a glossy appearance or improve the flavour. For instance, beaten egg or milk are used to glaze pastries and breads, and syrups or jams may be brushed over a cake top for an attractive finish.

Kneading
A process of pressing and stretching a dough, with your hands or a dough hook, to strengthen the gluten (the protein in wheat flour). This makes the gluten more elastic, enabling the dough to rise easily and giving an even texture to the finished product.

Knocking Back
This is a second kneading, usually done after the dough has been left to rise and before shaping, with the purpose of knocking out any large air bubbles from the dough, to ensure an even-textured result.

Piping
Forcing a soft cake or biscuit mixture, or an icing or frosting, from a piping bag through a nozzle, usually to create a decorative shape or effect, such as stars, rosettes or lines. Use a firm, even pressure for best results.

Proving
The leaving of a bread dough to rise after shaping, usually in a warm place. This is done to give the finished bread a good rise and a light, even texture.

Rubbing In
A method of incorporating fat, such as butter, into dry ingredients, such as flour, using the fingertips to rub the two together evenly. The fingertips are the coolest part of the hand, and a cool, light touch helps to give a short texture to pastry, scones and cakes.

Sifting
The shaking dry of ingredients, such as flour, through a sieve to eliminate lumps and give a smooth texture. It can also help to distribute any added raising agents or spices evenly through the mix.

Whipping
The gentle beating of a mixture, usually with a whisk, to make it smooth or to incorporate air. For example, it is used to thicken cream, or to make it stiff enough for piping.

Whisking
The rapid beating of a mixture using a hand whisk or electric whisk to incorporate and trap large amounts of air. This method is used for whisked sponge cakes, which rely totally on air for a light, open texture, and meringues, where the egg whites are whisked until they are stiff enough to hold peaks.

Chapter 1
Cakes

Victoria Sponge Cake

Serves 8–10

ingredients

- 175 g/6 oz butter, at room temperature, plus extra for greasing
- 175 g/6 oz caster sugar
- 3 eggs, beaten
- 175 g/6 oz self-raising flour
- pinch of salt
- 3 tbsp raspberry jam
- 1 tbsp caster or icing sugar

1 Preheat the oven to 180°C/350°F/ Gas Mark 4. Grease two 20-cm/ 8-inch sandwich cake tins and line with greaseproof paper or baking paper.

2 Cream the butter and sugar together in a mixing bowl using a wooden spoon or a hand-held mixer until the mixture is pale in colour and light and fluffy.

3 Add the eggs a little at a time, beating well after each addition. Sift the flour and salt and carefully add to the mixture, folding in with a metal spoon or a spatula. Divide the mixture between the tins and smooth over with the spatula.

4 Place them on the same shelf in the centre of the preheated oven and bake for 25–30 minutes until well risen, golden brown and beginning to shrink from the sides of the tin.

5 Remove from the oven and allow to stand for 1 minute. Loosen the cakes from around the edge of the tins using a palette knife. Turn the cakes out onto a clean tea towel, remove the paper and invert them onto a wire rack (this prevents the wire rack from marking the top of the cakes).

6 When completely cool, sandwich together with the jam and sprinkle with the sugar.

Orange & Poppy Seed
Bundt Cake

Serves 10

ingredients
- 200 g/7 oz unsalted butter, plus extra for greasing
- 200 g/7 oz golden caster sugar
- 3 large eggs, beaten
- finely grated rind of 1 orange
- 55 g/2 oz poppy seeds
- 300 g/10½ oz plain flour, plus extra for dusting
- 2 tsp baking powder
- 150 ml/5 fl oz milk
- 125 ml/4 fl oz orange juice
- strips of orange zest, to decorate

syrup
- 140 g/5 oz golden caster sugar
- 150 ml/5 fl oz orange juice

1 Preheat the oven to 160°C/325°F/ Gas Mark 3. Grease and lightly flour a Bundt ring tin, about 24 cm/ 9½ inches in diameter and with a capacity of approximately 2 litres/3½ pints.

2 Cream the butter and sugar together until pale and fluffy, then add the eggs gradually, beating thoroughly after each addition. Stir in the orange rind and poppy seeds. Sift in the flour and baking powder, then fold in evenly. Add the milk and orange juice, stirring to mix evenly.

3 Spoon the mixture into the prepared tin and bake in the preheated oven for 45–50 minutes, or until firm and golden brown. Leave to cool in the tin for 10 minutes, then turn out onto a wire rack to cool.

4 For the syrup, place the sugar and orange juice in a saucepan and heat gently until the sugar melts. Bring to the boil and simmer for about 5 minutes, until reduced and syrupy.

5 Spoon the syrup over the cake while it is still warm. Top with the strips of orange zest and serve warm or cold.

Double Chocolate Mint
Sponge

Serves 8

ingredients

- 150 g/5½ oz plain flour
- 2 tbsp cocoa powder
- 1 tbsp baking powder
- 175 g/6 oz unsalted butter, softened, plus extra for greasing
- 175 g/6 oz caster sugar
- 3 eggs, beaten
- 1 tbsp milk
- 40 g/1½ oz chocolate mint sticks, chopped
- 140 g/5 oz chocolate spread, plus extra to drizzle
- chocolate mint sticks to decorate

1 Preheat the oven to 180°C/350°F/ Gas Mark 4. Grease and line the bases of two 20-cm/8-inch sandwich cake tins.

2 Sift the flour, cocoa and baking powder into a bowl and beat in the butter, sugar and eggs, mixing until smooth. Stir in the milk and chocolate mint pieces.

3 Spread the mixture into the tins. Bake for 25–30 minutes in the preheated oven, until risen and firm. Cool in the tin for 2 minutes, then turn out and finish cooling on a wire rack.

4 Sandwich the cakes together with chocolate spread, then drizzle more chocolate spread over the top.

5 Decorate the cake with chocolate mint sticks.

Chocolate Fudge Cake

Serves 8

ingredients

- 175 g/6 oz unsalted butter, softened, plus extra for greasing
- 175 g/6 oz golden caster sugar
- 3 eggs, beaten
- 3 tbsp golden syrup
- 40 g/1½ oz ground almonds
- 175 g/6 oz self-raising flour
- pinch of salt
- 40 g/1½ oz cocoa powder

icing

- 225 g/8 oz plain chocolate, broken into pieces
- 55 g/2 oz dark muscovado sugar
- 225 g/8 oz unsalted butter, diced
- 5 tbsp evaporated milk
- ½ tsp vanilla extract

1 Preheat the oven to 180°C/350°F/ Gas Mark 4. Grease and line the bases of two 20-cm/8-inch sandwich cake tins.

2 To make the icing, place the chocolate, muscovado sugar, butter, evaporated milk and vanilla extract in a heavy-based saucepan. Heat gently, stirring constantly, until melted. Pour into a bowl and leave to cool. Cover and chill in the refrigerator for 1 hour, or until spreadable.

3 For the cake, place the butter and caster sugar in a bowl and beat together until light and fluffy. Gradually beat in the eggs. Stir in the golden syrup and ground almonds. Sift the flour, salt and cocoa powder into a separate bowl, then fold into the mixture. Add a little water, if necessary, to make a dropping consistency.

4 Spoon the mixture into the prepared tins and bake in the preheated oven for 30–35 minutes, or until springy to the touch and a skewer inserted in the centre comes out clean.

5 Leave the cakes in the tins for 5 minutes, then turn out onto a wire rack to cool completely. When the cakes are cold, sandwich them together with half the icing. Spread the remaining icing over the top and sides of the cake, swirling it to give a frosted appearance.

Coconut & Lime Cake

Serves 8

ingredients
- 175 g/6 oz unsalted butter, softened
- 175 g/6 oz caster sugar
- 3 eggs, beaten
- 150 g/5½ oz self-raising flour
- 85 g/3 oz desiccated coconut
- grated rind and juice of 1 lime

icing
- 175 g/6 oz icing sugar
- grated rind and juice of 1 lime
- 25 g/1 oz shredded coconut, lightly toasted

1 Preheat the oven to 160°C/325°F/Gas Mark 3. Grease a 20-cm/8-inch round cake tin and line with baking paper.

2 Place the butter and sugar in a large bowl and beat together until pale and fluffy. Gradually beat in the eggs. Sift in the flour and gently fold in using a metal spoon. Fold in the coconut, lime rind and juice.

3 Spoon the mixture into the prepared tin and level the surface. Bake in the preheated oven for 1–1¼ hours until risen, golden and firm to the touch. Cool in the tin for 5 minutes then turn out and cool completely on a wire rack.

4 For the icing, sift the icing sugar into a bowl. Stir in the lime rind and juice to make a thick smooth icing, adding a few drops of water, if necessary. Spoon the icing over the top of the cake, allowing it to drizzle down the sides of the cake. Scatter the toasted shredded coconut over the icing and leave to set.

Clementine Cake

Serves 8

ingredients
- 2 clementines
- 175 g/6 oz butter, softened, plus extra for greasing
- 175 g/6 oz caster sugar
- 3 eggs, beaten
- 175 g/6 oz self-raising flour
- 3 tbsp ground almonds
- 3 tbsp single cream

glaze & topping
- 6 tbsp clementine juice
- 2 tbsp caster sugar
- 3 white sugar cubes, crushed

1 Preheat the oven to 180°C/350°F/ Gas Mark 4. Grease an 18-cm/7-inch round cake tin with butter and line the base with baking paper.

2 Pare the rind from the clementines and chop the rind finely. In a bowl, cream together the butter, sugar and clementine rind until pale and fluffy.

3 Gradually add the beaten eggs to the mixture, beating thoroughly after each addition.

4 Gently fold in the self-raising flour followed by the ground almonds and the single cream. Spoon the mixture into the prepared tin.

5 Bake in the preheated oven for 55–60 minutes or until a fine skewer inserted into the centre comes out clean. Leave in the tin to cool slightly.

6 Meanwhile, make the glaze. Put the clementine juice into a small saucepan with the caster sugar. Bring to the boil and simmer for 5 minutes.

7 Transfer the cake to a wire rack. Drizzle the glaze over the cake until it has been absorbed and sprinkle with the crushed sugar cubes.

Classic Cherry Cake

Serves 8

ingredients

- 250 g/9 oz glacé cherries, quartered
- 85 g/3 oz ground almonds
- 200 g/7 oz plain flour
- 1 tsp baking powder
- 200 g/7 oz unsalted butter, plus extra for greasing
- 200 g/7 oz caster sugar
- 3 large eggs
- finely grated rind and juice of 1 lemon
- 6 sugar cubes, crushed

1 Preheat the oven to 180°C/350°F/ Gas Mark 4. Grease a 20-cm/8-inch round cake tin and line the base and sides with non-stick baking paper.

2 Stir together the cherries, ground almonds and 1 tablespoon of the flour in a bowl. Sift the remaining flour into a separate bowl with the baking powder.

3 Cream together the butter and sugar until light in colour and fluffy in texture. Gradually add the eggs, beating hard with each addition, until evenly mixed.

4 Add the flour and baking powder mixture and fold lightly and evenly into the creamed mixture with a metal spoon. Add the cherry mixture and fold in evenly. Finally, fold in the lemon rind and juice.

5 Spoon the mixture into the prepared cake tin and sprinkle with the crushed sugar cubes. Bake in the preheated oven for 1–1¼ hours, or until risen, golden brown and the cake is just beginning to shrink away from the sides of the tin.

6 Cool in the tin for about 15 minutes, then turn out to finish cooling on a wire rack.

Spiced Apple & Sultana Cake

Serves 8–10

ingredients

- 225 g/8 oz unsalted butter, softened, plus extra for greasing
- 225 g/8 oz light muscovado sugar
- 4 large eggs, lightly beaten
- 225 g/8 oz self-raising flour
- 2 tsp ground cinnamon
- ½ tsp grated nutmeg
- 85 g/3 oz sultanas
- 3 small dessert apples, peeled, cored and thinly sliced
- 2 tbsp clear honey, warmed

1 Preheat the oven to 180ºC/350ºF/ Gas Mark 4. Grease a 23-cm/9-inch round springform cake tin and line the base with baking paper.

2 Place the butter and sugar in a large bowl and beat together until light and fluffy. Gradually beat in the eggs. Sift the flour, cinnamon and nutmeg into the mixture and fold in gently using a metal spoon. Fold in the sultanas.

3 Spoon half the mixture into the prepared tin and level the surface. Scatter over half the sliced apples. Spoon over the rest of the cake mixture and gently level the surface. Arrange the rest of the apple slices over the top.

4 Bake in the preheated oven for 1–1¼ hours until risen, golden brown and firm to the touch. Leave to cool in the tin for 10 minutes then turn out to cool on a wire rack. Brush the top with the warmed honey and leave to cool completely.

Gingerbread

Serves 12–16

ingredients
- 450 g/1 lb plain flour
- 3 tsp baking powder
- 1 tsp bicarbonate of soda
- 3 tsp ground ginger
- 175 g/6 oz unsalted butter
- 175 g/6 oz soft brown sugar
- 175 g/6 oz black treacle
- 175 g/6 oz golden syrup
- 1 egg, beaten
- 300 ml/10 fl oz milk
- cream and warmed golden syrup, to serve

1 Line a 23-cm/9-inch square cake tin, 5 cm/2 inches deep, with greaseproof or baking paper. Preheat the oven to 160°C/325°F/Gas Mark 3.

2 Sift the flour, baking powder, bicarbonate of soda and ground ginger into a large mixing bowl.

3 Place the butter, sugar, treacle and syrup in a medium saucepan and heat over a low heat until the butter has melted and the sugar dissolved. Allow to cool a little. Mix the beaten egg with the milk and add to the cooled syrup mixture.

4 Add all the liquid ingredients to the flour mixture and beat well using a wooden spoon until the mixture is smooth and glossy.

5 Pour the mixture into the prepared tin and bake in the centre of the preheated oven for 1½ hours until well risen and just firm to the touch. This gives a lovely sticky gingerbread, but if you like a firmer cake cook for a further 15 minutes.

6 Remove from the oven and allow the cake to cool in the tin. When cool, remove the cake from the tin with the lining paper. Over wrap with foil and place in an airtight tin for up to 1 week to allow the flavours to mature.

7 Cut into wedges and serve cold with tea or coffee or warm with cream and golden syrup.

Sticky Toffee Pudding

Serves 6–8

ingredients
- 75 g/2¾ oz sultanas
- 150 g/5½ oz stoned dates, chopped
- 1 tsp bicarbonate of soda
- 25 g/1 oz butter, plus extra for greasing
- 200 g/7 oz soft light brown sugar
- 2 eggs
- 200 g/7 oz self-raising flour, sifted

sticky toffee sauce
- 25 g/1 oz butter
- 175 ml/6 fl oz double cream
- 200 g/7 oz soft light brown sugar

1 Preheat the oven to 180°C/350°F/ Gas Mark 4. Grease a 20-cm/8-inch round cake tin.

2 To make the pudding, put the sultanas, dates and bicarbonate of soda into a heatproof bowl. Cover with boiling water and leave to soak. Put the butter into a separate bowl, add the sugar and mix well. Beat in the eggs, then fold in the flour. Drain the soaked fruit, add to the bowl and mix.

3 Spoon the mixture evenly into the prepared cake tin. Bake in the preheated oven for 35–40 minutes, or until a skewer inserted into the centre comes out clean.

4 About 5 minutes before the end of the cooking time, make the sauce. Melt the butter in a saucepan over a medium heat. Stir in the cream and sugar and bring to the boil, stirring constantly. Reduce the heat and simmer for 5 minutes.

5 Turn out the pudding onto a wire rack for cooling. Leave for 5 minutes and then cut into slices and place on serving plates. Pour the sauce over each serving.

Polenta & Almond Cake

Serves 6

ingredients

- 200 g/7 oz unsalted butter, softened, plus extra for greasing
- 200 g/7 oz golden caster sugar
- juice and finely grated rind of 1 small orange
- 3 eggs, beaten
- 200 g/7 oz ground almonds
- 200 g/7 oz instant polenta
- 1 tsp baking powder
- vanilla ice cream, to serve

1 Preheat the oven to 180°C/350°F/ Gas Mark 4. Grease a 23-cm/9-inch round cake tin with a little of the butter and line the base with baking paper.

2 Beat together the remaining butter and the sugar with an electric mixer until pale and fluffy.

3 Add the orange juice and rind, eggs and almonds. Sift in the polenta and baking powder and beat until smooth.

4 Spread the mixture in the prepared tin, smoothing with a palette knife.

5 Bake in the preheated oven for 35–40 minutes, until firm and golden. Remove from the oven and leave to cool in the tin for 20 minutes.

6 Transfer the cake to a wire rack to cool. Cut the cake into slices and serve warm or cold with ice cream.

Stollen

Serves 10

ingredients

- 85 g/3 oz currants
- 55 g/2 oz raisins
- 35 g/1¼ oz chopped mixed peel
- 55 g/2 oz glacé cherries, rinsed, dried and quartered
- 2 tbsp dark rum
- 4 tbsp butter
- 175 ml/6 fl oz milk
- 3 tbsp golden caster sugar
- 375 g/13 oz strong white flour, plus extra for dusting
- ½ tsp salt
- ½ tsp grated nutmeg
- ½ tsp ground cinnamon
- seeds from 3 cardamom pods
- 2 tsp easy-blend dried yeast
- finely grated rind of 1 lemon
- 1 egg, beaten
- 40 g/1½ oz flaked almonds
- oil, for greasing
- 175 g/6 oz marzipan
- melted butter, for brushing
- icing sugar, for dredging

1 Put the currants, raisins, mixed peel and cherries in a bowl.

2 Stir in the rum and set aside. Put the butter, milk and caster sugar in a saucepan and heat gently until the sugar has dissolved and the butter has just melted. Leave to cool slightly.

3 Sift the flour, salt, nutmeg and cinnamon into a bowl. Crush the cardamom seeds and add them to the flour mixture. Stir in the yeast. Make a well in the centre and stir in the milk mixture, lemon rind and egg. Beat to form a soft dough.

4 Turn out the dough onto a floured work surface. With floured hands, knead the dough for about 5 minutes. It will be quite sticky, so add more flour if necessary. Knead the soaked fruit and flaked almonds into the dough until just combined. Place the dough in a clean, lightly oiled bowl. Cover with clingfilm and leave in a warm place for 1½ hours, or until doubled in size.

5 Turn the dough onto a floured work surface and knead lightly for 1–2 minutes, then roll out to a 25-cm/10-inch square.

6 Roll the marzipan into a sausage shape slightly shorter than the length of the dough and place down the centre. Fold one side over to cover the marzipan. Repeat with the other side, overlapping in the centre. Seal the ends. Place the roll, seam-side down, on a greased baking sheet. Cover with oiled clingfilm and leave in a warm place until doubled in size.

7 Preheat the oven to 190°C/375°F/Gas Mark 5. Remove the clingfilm and bake the stollen for 40 minutes, or until it is golden and it sounds hollow when tapped underneath.

8 Brush the hot stollen generously with melted butter and dredge heavily with icing sugar. Leave to cool on a wire rack.

Chocolate & Almond Layer Cake

Serves 10–12

ingredients
- 7 eggs
- 200 g/7 oz caster sugar
- 150 g/5½ oz plain flour
- 50 g/1¾ oz cocoa powder
- 50 g/1¾ oz butter, melted, plus extra for greasing

filling
- 200 g/7 oz dark chocolate
- 125 g/4½ oz butter
- 50 g/1¾ oz icing sugar

to decorate
- 75 g/2¾ oz toasted flaked almonds, crushed lightly
- grated chocolate

1 Preheat the oven to 180°C/350°F/ Gas Mark 4. Grease a deep 23-cm/ 9-inch square cake tin and line the base with baking paper.

2 Whisk the eggs and caster sugar in a mixing bowl with an electric whisk for about 10 minutes, or until the mixture is very light and foamy and the whisk leaves a trail that lasts a few seconds when lifted.

3 Sieve the flour and cocoa together and fold half into the mixture. Drizzle over the melted butter and fold in the rest of the flour and cocoa. Pour into the prepared tin and bake in the preheated oven for 30–35 minutes, or until springy to the touch. Leave to cool slightly, then remove from the tin and cool completely on a wire rack.

4 To make the filling, melt the chocolate and butter together, then remove from the heat. Stir in the icing sugar, leave to cool, then beat until thick enough to spread.

5 Halve the cake lengthways and cut each half into 3 layers. Sandwich the layers together with three quarters of the chocolate filling. Spread the remainder over the cake and mark a wavy pattern on the top. Press the almonds onto the sides. Decorate with grated chocolate.

Classic Carrot Cake

Serves 12

ingredients
- butter, for greasing
- 125 g/4½ oz self-raising flour
- pinch of salt
- 1 tsp ground cinnamon
- 125 g/4½ oz soft brown sugar
- 2 eggs
- 100 ml/3½ fl oz sunflower oil
- 125 g/4½ oz carrot, peeled and finely grated
- 25 g/1 oz desiccated coconut
- 25 g/1 oz walnuts, chopped
- walnut pieces, to decorate

icing
- 50 g/1¾ oz butter, softened
- 50 g/1¾ oz full-fat soft cheese
- 225 g/8 oz icing sugar, sifted
- 1 tsp lemon juice

1 Preheat the oven to 180°C/350°F/ Gas Mark 4. Lightly grease a 20-cm/ 8-inch square cake tin and line the base with baking paper.

2 Sift the flour, salt and ground cinnamon into a large bowl and stir in the brown sugar. Add the eggs and oil to the bowl and mix well.

3 Stir in the grated carrot, desiccated coconut and chopped walnuts.

4 Pour the mixture into the prepared tin and bake in the preheated oven for 20–25 minutes, or until just firm to the touch. Leave to cool in the tin.

5 Meanwhile, make the icing. In a bowl, beat together the butter, soft cheese, icing sugar and lemon juice until the mixture is fluffy and creamy.

6 Turn the cake out of the tin and cut into 12 bars or slices. Spread with the icing and then decorate with walnut pieces.

Banana Loaf

Serves 8

ingredients

- butter, for greasing
- 125 g/4½ oz white
  self-raising flour
- 100 g/3½ oz light brown
  self-raising flour
- 150 g/5½ oz demerara sugar
- pinch of salt
- ½ tsp ground cinnamon
- ½ grated nutmeg
- 2 large ripe bananas, peeled
- 175 ml/6 fl oz orange juice
- 2 eggs, beaten
- 4 tbsp rapeseed oil

1 Preheat the oven to 180°C/350°F/ Gas Mark 4. Lightly grease and line a 900-g/2-lb loaf tin.

2 Sift the flours, sugar, salt and the spices into a large bowl. In a separate bowl mash the bananas with the orange juice, then stir in the eggs and oil. Pour into the dry ingredients and mix well.

3 Spoon into the prepared tin and bake in the preheated oven for 1 hour. Test to see if the loaf is cooked by inserting a skewer into the centre. If it comes out clean, the loaf is done. If not, bake for a further 10 minutes and test again.

4 Remove from the oven and leave to cool in the tin. Turn out the loaf onto a wire rack, slice and serve.

Butternut Squash & Orange
Cake

Serves 10–12

ingredients

- 175 g/6 oz butter, softened, plus extra for greasing
- 175 g/6 oz light soft brown sugar
- 3 eggs, beaten
- finely grated zest and juice of 1 orange
- 225 g/8 oz self-raising wholemeal flour
- 1 tsp baking powder
- 1 tsp ground cinnamon
- 225 g/8 oz prepared butternut squash flesh (peeled and seeded weight), coarsely grated
- 115 g/4 oz sultanas

topping

- 225 g/8 oz full-fat soft cheese
- 55 g/2 oz icing sugar, sifted
- 1 tsp finely grated orange zest (reserved from cake ingredients)
- 2–3 tsp freshly squeezed orange juice (reserved from cake ingredients)
- thinly pared orange zest, to decorate

1 Preheat the oven to 180°C/350°F/ Gas Mark 4. Grease and line a deep 18-cm/7-inch round cake tin with baking paper.

2 For the cake, cream the butter and sugar together in a bowl until light and fluffy. Gradually beat in the eggs, beating well after each addition. Reserve 1 teaspoon of orange zest for the topping, then beat the remaining orange zest into the creamed mixture.

3 Fold in the flour, baking powder and cinnamon, then fold in the squash, sultanas and a little orange juice, if necessary (about 1 tablespoon) to give a fairly soft consistency. Spoon the mixture into the prepared tin and level the surface.

4 Bake in the preheated oven for about 1 hour or until risen, firm to the touch and deep golden brown. Remove from the oven and cool in the tin for a few minutes, then turn out onto a wire rack. Remove the lining paper and leave to cool completely.

5 To make the topping, beat the soft cheese, icing sugar, reserved grated orange zest and 2–3 teaspoons of reserved orange juice together in a bowl until smooth and combined. Spread over the top of the cold cake, swirling it attractively, then sprinkle with pared orange zest. Serve immediately in slices.

Lemon Drizzle Cake

Serves 8

ingredients
- butter, for greasing
- 200 g/7 oz plain flour
- 2 tsp baking powder
- 200 g/7 oz caster sugar
- 4 eggs
- 150 ml/5 fl oz soured cream
- grated rind of 1 large lemon
- 4 tbsp lemon juice
- 150 ml/5 fl oz sunflower oil

syrup
- 4 tbsp icing sugar
- 3 tbsp lemon juice

1 Preheat the oven to 180°C/350°F/ Gas Mark 4. Lightly grease a 20-cm/ 8-inch loose-bottomed round cake tin and line the base with baking paper.

2 Sieve the flour and baking powder into a mixing bowl and stir in the caster sugar.

3 In a separate bowl, whisk the eggs, soured cream, lemon rind, lemon juice and oil together.

4 Pour the egg mixture into the dry ingredients and mix well until evenly combined.

5 Pour the mixture into the prepared tin and bake in the preheated oven for 45–60 minutes until risen and golden brown.

6 Meanwhile, to make the syrup, mix together the icing sugar and lemon juice in a small saucepan. Stir over a low heat until just beginning to bubble and turn syrupy.

7 As soon as the cake comes out of the oven, prick the surface with a fine skewer, then brush the syrup over the top. Leave the cake to cool completely in the tin before turning out and serving.

Double Chocolate Gateau

Serves 10

ingredients
- 225 g/8 oz butter, softened, plus extra for greasing
- 225 g/8 oz golden caster sugar
- 4 eggs, beaten
- 225 g/8 oz self-raising flour
- 55 g/2 oz cocoa powder
- a little milk (optional)

filling
- 250 ml/9 fl oz whipping cream
- 225 g/8 oz white chocolate, broken into pieces

icing
- 350 g/12 oz plain chocolate, broken into pieces
- 115 g/4 oz butter
- 100 ml/3½ fl oz double cream

to decorate
- 115 g/4 oz plain chocolate caraque
- 2 tsp icing sugar and cocoa powder, mixed

1 To make the filling, put the whipping cream in a saucepan and heat to almost boiling. Put the white chocolate in a food processor and chop. With the motor running, pour the hot cream through the feed tube and process for 10–15 seconds, until smooth. Transfer to a bowl, leave to cool, then cover with clingfilm and chill in the refrigerator for 2 hours, or until firm. Whisk until just starting to hold soft peaks.

2 Preheat the oven to 180°C/350°F/ Gas Mark 4. Grease and line the base of a 20-cm/8-inch round deep cake tin with baking paper.

3 Put the butter and sugar in a bowl and beat until light and fluffy. Gradually beat in the eggs. Sift the flour and cocoa into a bowl, then fold into the mixture, adding milk, if necessary, to make a dropping consistency.

4 Spoon into the prepared tin and bake in the preheated oven for 45–50 minutes, until a skewer inserted into the centre comes out clean. Leave to stand in the tin for 5 minutes. Transfer to a wire rack to cool completely.

5 To make the icing, put the plain chocolate in a heatproof bowl set over a saucepan of gently simmering water until melted. Stir in the butter and double cream. Leave to cool, stirring occasionally until the mixture is a thick spreading consistency.

6 Slice the cake horizontally into three layers. Sandwich the layers together with the white chocolate filling. Cover the top and sides of the cake with the icing and arrange the chocolate caraque over the top. Sift the mixed icing sugar and cocoa over the cake.

White Chocolate Coffee
Gateau

Serves 8–10

ingredients
- 40 g/1½ oz unsalted butter,
  plus extra for greasing
- 85 g/3 oz white chocolate
- 125 g/4½ oz caster sugar
- 4 large eggs, beaten
- 2 tbsp very strong black coffee
- 1 tsp vanilla extract
- 125 g/4½ oz plain flour
- white chocolate curls,
  to decorate

frosting
- 175 g/6 oz white chocolate
- 85 g/3 oz unsalted butter
- 125 g/4½ oz crème fraîche
- 125 g/4½ oz icing sugar, sifted
- 1 tbsp coffee liqueur or very
  strong black coffee

1 Preheat the oven to 180°C/350°F/
Gas Mark 4. Grease two 20-cm/8-inch
sandwich cake tins and line the bases with
baking paper.

2 Place the butter and chocolate in a bowl
set over a saucepan of hot, but not
simmering, water and leave on a very low
heat until just melted. Stir to mix lightly, then
remove from the heat.

3 Place the caster sugar, eggs, coffee and
vanilla extract in a large bowl set over a
saucepan of hot water and whisk hard with
an electric whisk until the mixture is pale
and thick enough to leave a trail when the
whisk is lifted.

4 Remove from the heat, sift in the flour
and fold in lightly and evenly. Quickly
fold in the butter and chocolate mixture,
then divide the mixture between the
prepared tins.

5 Bake in the preheated oven for
25–30 minutes, until risen, golden
brown and springy to the touch. Leave to
cool in the tins for 2 minutes, then run a
knife around the edges to loosen and turn
out onto a wire rack to cool.

6 For the frosting, place the chocolate
and butter in a bowl set over a
saucepan of hot water and heat gently until
melted. Remove from the heat, stir in the
crème fraîche, then add the icing sugar and
coffee liqueur and mix until smooth. Chill
the frosting for at least 30 minutes, stirring
occasionally, until it becomes thick and
glossy.

7 Use about one third of the frosting to
sandwich the cakes together. Spread
the remainder over the top and sides,
swirling with a palette knife. Arrange the
chocolate curls over the top of the cake
and leave to set.

Chapter 2
Small Cakes & Bars

Vanilla Macaroons

Makes 16

ingredients
- 75 g/2¾ oz ground almonds
- 115 g/4 oz icing sugar
- 2 large egg whites
- 50 g/1¾ oz caster sugar
- ½ tsp vanilla extract

filling
- 55 g/2 oz unsalted butter, softened
- ½ tsp vanilla extract
- 115 g/4 oz icing sugar, sifted

1 Place the ground almonds and icing sugar in a food processor and process for 15 seconds. Sift the mixture into a bowl. Line two baking sheets with baking paper.

2 Place the egg whites in a large bowl and whisk until holding soft peaks. Gradually whisk in the caster sugar to make a firm, glossy meringue. Whisk in the vanilla extract.

3 Using a spatula, fold the almond mixture into the meringue one third at a time. When all the dry ingredients are thoroughly incorporated, continue to cut and fold the mixture until it forms a shiny batter with a thick, ribbon-like consistency.

4 Pour the mixture into a piping bag fitted with a 1-cm/½-inch plain nozzle. Pipe 32 small rounds onto the prepared baking sheets. Tap the baking sheets firmly onto a work surface to remove air bubbles. Leave at room temperature for 30 minutes. Preheat the oven to 160°C/325°F/ Gas Mark 3.

5 Bake in the preheated oven for 10–15 minutes. Cool for 10 minutes, then carefully peel the macaroons off the baking paper. Leave to cool completely.

6 To make the filling, beat the butter and vanilla extract in a bowl until pale and fluffy. Gradually beat in the icing sugar until smooth and creamy. Use to sandwich pairs of macaroons together.

Hazelnut Chocolate
Macaroons

Makes 16

ingredients

- 50 g/1¾ oz ground almonds
- 25 g/1 oz hazelnuts, finely ground, plus 1 tbsp chopped for decoration
- 115 g/4 oz icing sugar
- 2 large egg whites
- 50 g/1¾ oz caster sugar
- 6 tbsp hazelnut and chocolate spread

1 Place the ground almonds, ground hazelnuts and icing sugar in a food processor and process for 15 seconds. Sift the mixture into a bowl. Line two baking sheets with baking paper.

2 Place the egg whites in a large bowl and whisk until holding soft peaks. Gradually whisk in the caster sugar until you have a firm, glossy meringue.

3 Using a spatula, fold the almond mixture into the meringue one third at a time. When all the dry ingredients are thoroughly incorporated, continue to cut and fold the mixture until it forms a shiny batter with a thick, ribbon-like consistency.

4 Pour the mixture into a piping bag fitted with a 1-cm/½-inch plain nozzle. Pipe 32 small rounds onto the prepared baking sheets. Tap the baking sheets firmly onto a work surface to remove air bubbles. Sprinkle over the chopped hazelnuts. Leave at room temperature for 30 minutes. Preheat the oven to 160°C/325°F/ Gas Mark 3.

5 Bake in the preheated oven for 10–15 minutes. Cool for 10 minutes, then carefully peel the macaroons off the baking paper. Leave to cool completely.

6 Sandwich pairs of macaroons together with the hazelnut and chocolate spread.

Double Chocolate Muffins

Makes 12

ingredients

- 100 g/3½ oz butter, softened
- 125 g/4½ oz caster sugar
- 100 g/3½ oz dark muscovado sugar
- 2 eggs
- 150 ml/5 fl oz soured cream
- 5 tbsp milk
- 250 g/9 oz plain flour
- 1 tsp bicarbonate of soda
- 2 tbsp cocoa powder
- 190 g/6½ oz plain chocolate chips

1 Preheat the oven to 190°C/375°F/ Gas Mark 5. Line a 12-hole muffin tin with paper cases.

2 Put the butter, caster sugar and muscovado sugar into a bowl and beat well. Beat in the eggs, soured cream and milk until thoroughly mixed.

3 Sift the flour, bicarbonate of soda and cocoa powder into a separate bowl and stir into the mixture. Add the chocolate chips and mix well.

4 Spoon the mixture into the paper cases. Bake in the preheated oven for 25–30 minutes. Remove from the oven and leave to cool for 10 minutes. Turn out onto a wire rack and leave to cool completely.

Warm Spiced Apple Pie
Cupcakes

Makes 12

ingredients
- 50 g/1¾ oz butter, softened
- 70 g/2½ oz demerara sugar
- 1 egg, lightly beaten
- 150 g/5½ oz plain flour
- 1½ tsp baking powder
- ½ tsp ground mixed spice
- 1 large cooking apple, peeled, cored and finely chopped
- 1 tbsp orange juice

topping
- 40 g/1½ oz plain flour
- ½ tsp ground mixed spice
- 25 g/1 oz butter
- 40 g/1½ oz caster sugar

1 Preheat the oven to 180°C/350°F/Gas Mark 4. Line a 12-hole muffin tin with 12 paper cases.

2 To make the topping, place the flour, mixed spice, butter and sugar in a large bowl and rub in with your fingertips until the mixture resembles fine breadcrumbs. Set aside.

3 To make the cupcakes, place the butter and sugar in a large bowl and beat together until light and fluffy, then gradually beat in the egg. Sift in the flour, baking powder and mixed spice and fold into the mixture, then fold in the chopped apple and orange juice. Spoon the mixture into the paper cases. Add the topping to cover the top of each cupcake and press down gently.

4 Bake in the preheated oven for 30 minutes, or until golden brown. Leave the cupcakes to cool in the tin for 2–3 minutes and serve warm, or leave to cool for 10 minutes and then transfer to a wire rack to cool completely.

Vanilla Frosted Cupcakes

Makes 12

ingredients

- 115 g/4 oz unsalted butter, softened
- 115 g/4 oz golden caster sugar
- 2 eggs, lightly beaten
- 115 g/4 oz self-raising flour
- 1 tbsp milk
- crystallized rose petals, to decorate

frosting

- 175 g/6 oz unsalted butter, softened
- 2 tsp vanilla extract
- 2 tbsp milk
- 300 g/10½ oz icing sugar, sifted

1 Preheat the oven to 180°C/350°F/ Gas Mark 4. Line a 12-hole muffin tin with paper cases.

2 Place the butter and sugar in a bowl and beat together until light and fluffy. Gradually beat in the eggs. Sift in the flour and fold in gently using a metal spoon. Fold in the milk.

3 Spoon the mixture into the paper cases. Bake in the preheated oven for 15–20 minutes until golden brown and firm to the touch. Transfer to a wire rack and leave to cool.

4 To make the frosting, put the butter, vanilla extract and milk in a large bowl. Using an electric hand-held whisk beat the mixture until smooth. Gradually beat in the icing sugar and continue beating for 2–3 minutes until the frosting is very light and creamy.

5 Spoon the frosting into a large piping bag fitted with a large star nozzle and pipe swirls of the frosting onto the top of each cupcake. Decorate each cupcake with crystallized rose petals.

Chocolate Chip Brownies

Makes 12

ingredients

- 150 g/5½ oz plain chocolate, broken into pieces
- 225 g/8 oz butter, softened, plus extra for greasing
- 225 g/8 oz self-raising flour
- 125 g/4½ oz caster sugar
- 4 eggs, beaten
- 75 g/2¾ oz pistachio nuts, chopped
- 100 g/3½ oz white chocolate, roughly chopped
- icing sugar, for dusting

1 Preheat the oven to 180°C/350°F/ Gas Mark 4. Grease a 23-cm/9-inch square baking tin and line with baking paper.

2 Place the chocolate and softened butter in a heatproof bowl set over a saucepan of simmering water. Stir until melted, then leave to cool slightly.

3 Sift the flour into a separate bowl and stir in the caster sugar.

4 Stir the beaten eggs into the chocolate mixture, then pour the mixture into the flour and sugar and beat well. Stir in the pistachio nuts and white chocolate, then pour the mixture into the tin, using a palette knife to spread it evenly.

5 Bake in the preheated oven for 30–35 minutes, or until firm to the touch around the edges. Leave to cool in the tin for 20 minutes. Turn out onto a wire rack. Dust with icing sugar and leave to cool completely. Cut into 12 pieces and serve.

Rocky Road Brownies

Makes 16

ingredients

- 100 g/3½ oz plain flour, plus extra for dusting
- 140 g/5 oz caster sugar
- 3 tbsp cocoa powder
- ½ tsp baking powder
- 225 g/8 oz butter, melted, plus extra for greasing
- 2 eggs, beaten
- 1 tsp vanilla extract
- 70 g/2½ oz glacé cherries, quartered
- 70 g/2½ oz blanched almonds, chopped
- 100 g/3½ oz marshmallows, chopped

fudge frosting

- 200 g/7 oz icing sugar
- 2 tbsp cocoa powder
- 3 tbsp evaporated milk
- ½ tsp vanilla extract

1 Preheat the oven to 160°C/325°F/ Gas Mark 3. Grease a 23-cm/9-inch square shallow baking tin and dust lightly with flour.

2 Sift together the flour, sugar, cocoa and baking powder and make a well in the centre. Stir in the melted butter, eggs and vanilla extract and beat well to mix thoroughly.

3 Stir in the cherries and almonds. Pour into the prepared tin and bake for 35–40 minutes in the preheated oven, until just firm on top. Leave to cool in the tin.

4 Meanwhile, make the frosting. Place all the ingredients in a large bowl and beat well to mix to a smooth, just spreadable consistency.

5 Spread the cooled brownies with the frosting, swirling lightly, and sprinkle with marshmallows. Leave until the frosting sets, then cut into squares.

Lamington Cakes

Makes 16

ingredients
- 6 eggs
- 150 g/5½ oz caster sugar
- 175 g/6 oz plain flour
- 55 g/2 oz unsalted butter, melted, plus extra for greasing
- 250 g/9 oz desiccated coconut

icing
- 500 g/1 lb 2 oz icing sugar
- 40 g/1½ oz cocoa powder
- 85 ml/3 fl oz boiling water
- 75 g/2¾ oz unsalted butter, melted

1 Preheat the oven to 180°C/350°F/ Gas Mark 4. Grease a 20-cm/8-inch square cake tin and line the base with baking paper.

2 Place the eggs and caster sugar in a large bowl set over a saucepan of gently simmering water and whisk until pale and thick enough to leave a trail when the whisk is lifted.

3 Remove from the heat, sift in the flour and fold in evenly. Fold in the melted butter. Pour into the prepared tin and bake in the preheated oven for 35–40 minutes, or until risen, golden and springy to the touch.

4 Leave to cool in the tin for 2–3 minutes, then turn out on to a wire rack to finish cooling. When cold, cut the cake into 16 squares.

5 For the icing, sift the icing sugar and cocoa together into a bowl and stir in the water and butter, mixing until smooth. Spread out the desiccated coconut on a large plate. Dip each piece of sponge cake into the icing, using two palette knives to turn and coat evenly. Place in the desiccated coconut and turn to coat evenly. Put the cakes on a sheet of baking paper and leave to set.

Malted Chocolate Bars

Makes 16

ingredients

- 85 g/3 oz butter, plus extra for greasing
- 2 tbsp golden syrup
- 2 tbsp malted chocolate powder
- 225 g/8 oz malted milk biscuits
- 75 g/2¾ oz milk or plain chocolate, broken into pieces
- 2 tbsp icing sugar
- 2 tbsp milk

1 Grease and line the bottom of a shallow 18-cm/7-inch round cake tin or flan tin.

2 Place the butter, golden syrup and malted chocolate powder in a small saucepan and heat gently, stirring all the time until the butter has melted and the mixture is well combined.

3 Crush the biscuits in a polythene bag with a rolling pin, or process them in a food processor. Stir the biscuit crumbs into the chocolate mixture and mix well.

4 Press the mixture into the prepared tin and then chill in the refrigerator until firm.

5 Place the chocolate pieces in a small heatproof bowl with the sugar and the milk. Place the bowl over a saucepan of gently simmering water and stir until the chocolate melts and the mixture is combined.

6 Spread the chocolate icing over the biscuit base and let the icing set in the tin. Using a sharp knife, cut into bars to serve.

Macadamia Nut Caramel Squares

Makes 16

ingredients
- 115 g/4 oz macadamia nuts
- 280 g/10 oz plain flour
- 175 g/6 oz soft brown sugar
- 115 g/4 oz butter

topping
- 115 g/4 oz butter
- 100 g/3½ oz soft brown sugar
- 200 g/7 oz milk chocolate chips

1 Preheat the oven to 180°C/350°F/ Gas Mark 4.

2 Roughly chop the macadamia nuts. To make the base, beat together the flour, sugar and butter until the mixture resembles fine breadcrumbs.

3 Press the mixture into the bottom of a 30 x 20-cm/12 x 8-inch rectangular baking tin. Sprinkle over the macadamia nuts.

4 To make the topping, put the butter and sugar in a saucepan and, stirring constantly, slowly bring the mixture to the boil. Boil for 1 minute, stirring constantly, then carefully pour the mixture over the macadamia nuts.

5 Bake in the preheated oven for about 20 minutes, until the caramel topping is bubbling. Remove from the oven and immediately sprinkle the chocolate chips evenly on top. Leave for 2–3 minutes, until the chocolate chips start to melt then, using the blade of a knife, swirl the chocolate over the top. Leave to cool in the tin, then cut into squares.

Chocolate Caramel
Shortbread

Makes 12

ingredients

- 115 g/4 oz butter, plus extra for greasing
- 175 g/6 oz plain flour
- 55 g/2 oz golden caster sugar

filling & topping

- 175 g/6 oz butter
- 115 g/4 oz golden caster sugar
- 3 tbsp golden syrup
- 400 g/14 oz canned condensed milk
- 200 g/7 oz plain chocolate, broken into pieces

1 Preheat the oven to 180°C/350°F/ Gas Mark 4. Grease and line the base of a 23-cm/9-inch shallow square cake tin.

2 Place the butter, flour and sugar in a food processor and process until it begins to bind together. Press the mixture into the prepared tin and smooth the top. Bake in the preheated oven for 20–25 minutes, or until golden.

3 Meanwhile, make the filling. Place the butter, sugar, golden syrup and condensed milk in a saucepan and heat gently until the sugar has dissolved. Bring to the boil and simmer for 6–8 minutes, stirring constantly, until the mixture becomes very thick. Pour over the shortbread base and leave to chill in the refrigerator until firm.

4 To make the topping, melt the chocolate and leave to cool, then spread over the caramel. Chill in the refrigerator until set. Cut the shortbread into 12 pieces with a sharp knife and serve.

Almond Biscotti

Makes about 35

ingredients
- 250 g/9 oz whole blanched almonds
- 200 g/7 oz plain flour, plus extra for dusting
- 175 g/6 oz caster sugar, plus extra for sprinkling
- 1 tsp baking powder
- ½ tsp ground cinnamon
- 2 eggs
- 2 tsp vanilla extract

1 Preheat the oven to 180°C/350°F/ Gas Mark 4. Line two baking sheets with baking paper.

2 Very roughly chop the almonds, leaving some whole. Mix the flour, sugar, baking powder and cinnamon together in a mixing bowl. Stir in the almonds.

3 Beat the eggs with the vanilla extract in a small bowl, then add to the flour mixture and mix together to form a firm dough. Turn the dough out onto a lightly floured surface and knead lightly.

4 Divide the dough in half and shape each piece into a log, roughly 5 cm/2 inches wide. Transfer to the prepared baking sheets and sprinkle with sugar. Bake in the preheated oven for 20–25 minutes, until firm.

5 Remove from the oven and leave to cool slightly, then transfer to a chopping board and cut into 1-cm/½-inch slices. Meanwhile, reduce the oven temperature to 160°C/325°F/Gas Mark 3.

6 Arrange the slices, cut-sides down, on the baking sheets. Bake in the oven for 15–20 minutes, until dry and crisp. Transfer to a wire rack to cool. Store in an airtight container to keep crisp.

Nutty Flapjacks

Makes 16

ingredients
- 200 g/7 oz rolled oats
- 115 g/4 oz chopped hazelnuts
- 55 g/2 oz plain flour
- 115 g/4 oz butter,
  plus extra for greasing
- 2 tbsp golden syrup
- 85 g/3 oz light muscovado sugar

1 Preheat the oven to 180°C/350°F/ Gas Mark 4, then grease a 23-cm/ 9-inch square ovenproof dish or cake tin. Place the rolled oats, chopped hazelnuts and flour in a large mixing bowl and stir together.

2 Place the butter, syrup and sugar in a saucepan over a low heat and stir until melted. Pour onto the dry ingredients and mix well. Turn the mixture into the prepared ovenproof dish and smooth the surface with the back of a spoon.

3 Bake in the preheated oven for 20–25 minutes, or until golden and firm to the touch. Mark into 16 pieces and leave to cool in the tin. When completely cooled, cut through with a sharp knife and remove from the tin.

Chocolate Peanut Butter
Squares

Makes 20

ingredients

- 300 g/10½ oz milk chocolate
- 350 g/12 oz plain flour
- 1 tsp baking powder
- 225 g/8 oz butter
- 350 g/12 oz soft light brown sugar
- 175 g/6 oz rolled oats
- 70 g/2½ oz chopped mixed nuts
- 1 egg, beaten
- 400 g/14 oz canned condensed milk
- 70 g/2½ oz crunchy peanut butter

1 Preheat the oven to 180°C/350°F/ Gas Mark 4.

2 Finely chop the chocolate. Sift the flour and baking powder into a large bowl. Add the butter to the flour mixture and rub in using your fingertips until the mixture resembles breadcrumbs. Stir in the sugar, rolled oats and nuts.

3 Put a quarter of the mixture into a bowl and stir in the chopped chocolate. Set aside.

4 Stir the egg into the remaining mixture, then press into the base of a 30 x 20-cm/12 x 8-inch baking tin. Bake in the preheated oven for 15 minutes. Meanwhile, mix the condensed milk and peanut butter together. Pour the mixture over the base and spread evenly, then sprinkle the reserved chocolate mixture on top and press down lightly.

5 Return to the oven and bake for a further 20 minutes, until golden brown. Leave to cool in the tin, then cut into squares.

White Chocolate & Apricot Squares

Makes 12

ingredients

- 125 g/4½ oz butter, plus extra for greasing
- 175 g/6 oz white chocolate, chopped
- 4 eggs
- 100 g/3½ oz caster sugar
- 250 g/9 oz plain flour, sifted
- 1 tsp baking powder
- pinch of salt
- 100 g/3½ oz ready-to-eat dried apricots, chopped

1 Preheat the oven to 180°C/350°F/Gas Mark 4. Lightly grease a 20-cm/8-inch square cake tin and line the bottom with a sheet of baking paper.

2 Melt the butter and chocolate in a heatproof bowl set over a saucepan of gently simmering water. Stir frequently with a wooden spoon until the mixture is smooth and glossy. Leave the mixture to cool slightly.

3 Beat the eggs and caster sugar into the butter and chocolate mixture until well combined.

4 Fold in the flour, baking powder, salt and chopped dried apricots and mix thoroughly.

5 Pour the mixture into the tin and bake in the preheated oven for about 25–30 minutes. The centre of the cake may not be completely firm, but it will set as it cools. Leave in the tin to cool.

6 When the cake is completely cold, turn it out carefully and slice into bars or small squares.

Viennese Jam Shortcakes

Makes 12

ingredients

- 225 g/8 oz unsalted butter, softened
- 1 tsp vanilla extract
- 85 g/3 oz icing sugar, plus extra for dusting
- 175 g/6 oz self-raising flour
- 55 g/2 oz cornflour
- 2 tbsp strawberry jam

1 Preheat the oven to 180°C/350°F/ Gas Mark 4. Line a 12-hole muffin tin with paper cases.

2 Place the butter and vanilla extract in a large bowl and using an electric hand-held whisk beat together until the butter is very soft. Sift in the icing sugar and beat thoroughly.

3 Sift together the flour and cornflour and stir into the mixture until smooth. Spoon the mixture into a large piping bag fitted with a large star nozzle and pipe swirls of the mixture into the paper cases, leaving a slight dip in the centre of each one.

4 Bake in the preheated oven for 15–20 minutes until golden. Leave the shortcakes in the tray for 15 minutes then transfer to a wire rack and leave to cool completely.

5 Spoon a little jam into the centre of each shortcake and dust with icing sugar.

Chocolate Whoopie Pies

Makes 10

ingredients
- 175 g/6 oz plain flour
- 1½ tsp bicarbonate of soda
- 40 g/1½ oz cocoa powder
- large pinch of salt
- 85 g/3 oz butter, softened
- 85 g/3 oz white vegetable fat
- 150 g/5½ oz soft dark brown sugar
- 1 large egg, beaten
- 1 tsp vanilla extract
- 150 ml/5 fl oz milk

marshmallow filling
- 225 g/8 oz white marshmallows
- 4 tbsp milk
- 115 g/4 oz white vegetable fat
- 55 g/2 oz icing sugar, sifted

1 Preheat the oven to 180°C/350°F/ Gas Mark 4. Line 2–3 large baking sheets with baking paper. Sift together the plain flour, bicarbonate of soda, cocoa powder and salt.

2 Place the butter, white vegetable fat and sugar in a large bowl and beat with an electric hand-held whisk until pale and fluffy. Beat in the egg and vanilla extract followed by half the flour mixture and then the milk. Stir in the rest of the flour mixture and mix until thoroughly incorporated.

3 Pipe or spoon 18 mounds of the mixture onto the prepared baking sheets, spaced well apart to allow for spreading. Bake in the preheated oven, one sheet at a time, for 12–14 minutes until risen and just firm to the touch. Cool for 5 minutes, then using a palette knife transfer to a cooling rack and leave to cool completely.

4 For the filling, place the marshmallows and milk in a heatproof bowl set over a pan of simmering water. Leave until the marshmallows have melted, stirring occasionally. Remove from the heat and leave to cool.

5 Place the white vegetable fat and icing sugar in a bowl and beat together until smooth and creamy. Add the creamed mixture to the marshmallow and beat for 1–2 minutes until fluffy.

6 To assemble, spread the filling over the flat side of half the cakes. Top with the remaining cakes.

Hazelnut Bars

Makes 16

ingredients
- 150 g/5½ oz plain flour
- pinch of salt
- 1 tsp baking powder
- 100 g/3½ oz butter, cut into small pieces, plus extra for greasing
- 150 g/5½ oz soft brown sugar
- 1 egg, beaten
- 4 tbsp milk
- 100 g/3½ oz hazelnuts, halved
- demerara sugar, for sprinkling (optional)

1 Preheat the oven to 180°C/350°F/ Gas Mark 4. Grease a 23-cm/9-inch square cake tin and line the base with baking paper.

2 Sieve the flour, salt and baking powder into a large mixing bowl. Rub in the butter with your fingers until the mixture resembles fine breadcrumbs. Stir in the brown sugar.

3 Add the egg, milk and nuts to the mixture and stir well until thoroughly combined.

4 Spoon the mixture into the prepared cake tin and level the surface. Sprinkle with demerara sugar, if using.

5 Bake in the preheated oven for about 25 minutes, or until the mixture is firm to the touch when pressed with a finger.

6 Leave to cool for 10 minutes, then loosen the edges with a round-bladed knife and turn out onto a wire rack. Cut into squares.

Date, Pistachio & Honey
Slices

Makes 12 slices

ingredients
- 250 g/9 oz stoned dates, chopped
- 2 tbsp lemon juice
- 2 tbsp water
- 85 g/3 oz pistachio nuts, chopped
- 2 tbsp clear honey
- milk to glaze

pastry
- 225 g/8 oz plain flour, plus extra for dusting
- 25 g/1 oz golden caster sugar
- 150 g/5½ oz butter
- 4–5 tbsp cold water to mix

1 Place the dates, lemon juice and water in a saucepan and bring to the boil, stirring. Remove from the heat. Stir in the pistachios and 1 tablespoon of honey. Cover and leave to cool.

2 Preheat the oven to 200°C/400°F/ Gas Mark 6. For the pastry, place the flour, sugar and butter in a food processor and process to fine breadcrumbs.

3 Mix in just enough cold water to bind to a soft, not sticky, dough. Roll out the pastry on a floured surface to two 30 x 20-cm/12 x 8-inch rectangles. Place one on a baking sheet.

4 Spread the date and nut mixture to within 1 cm/½ inch of the edge. Top with the remaining pastry. Press to seal, trim the edges and mark into 12 slices. Glaze with milk.

5 Bake in the preheated oven for 20–25 minutes, until golden. Brush with the remaining honey and cool on a wire rack. Cut into 12 slices and serve.

Chapter 3
Cookies & Biscuits

Chocolate Chip Cookies

Makes 18

ingredients

- 125 g/4½ oz soft margarine, plus extra for greasing
- 175 g/6 oz plain flour
- 1 tsp baking powder
- 85 g/3 oz light muscovado sugar
- 5 tbsp caster sugar
- ½ tsp vanilla extract
- 1 egg
- 125 g/4½ oz dark chocolate chips

1 Preheat the oven to 190°C/375°F/ Gas Mark 5. Lightly grease two baking sheets.

2 Place all of the ingredients in a large mixing bowl and beat until well combined.

3 Place tablespoonfuls of the mixture onto the baking sheets, spacing them well apart to allow for spreading during cooking.

4 Bake in the preheated oven for 10–12 minutes or until the cookies are golden brown.

5 Using a palette knife, transfer the cookies to a wire rack to cool completely before serving.

Classic Oatmeal Cookies

Makes 30

ingredients

- 175 g/6 oz butter or margarine, plus extra for greasing
- 275 g/9¾ oz demerara sugar
- 1 egg
- 4 tbsp water
- 1 tsp vanilla extract
- 375 g/13 oz rolled oats
- 140 g/5 oz plain flour
- 1 tsp salt
- ½ tsp bicarbonate of soda

1 Preheat the oven to 180°C/350°F/ Gas Mark 4 and grease a large baking sheet.

2 Cream the butter and sugar together in a large mixing bowl. Beat in the egg, water and vanilla extract until the mixture is smooth. In a separate bowl, mix the oats, flour, salt and bicarbonate of soda.

3 Gradually stir the oat mixture into the creamed mixture until thoroughly combined.

4 Place tablespoonfuls of the mixture onto the prepared baking sheet, making sure they are well spaced. Transfer to the preheated oven and bake for 15 minutes, or until the cookies are golden brown.

5 Remove the cookies from the oven and place on a wire rack to cool before serving.

Peanut Butter Biscuits

Makes 26

ingredients

- 115 g/4 oz butter, softened, plus extra for greasing
- 115 g/4 oz crunchy peanut butter
- 115 g/4 oz golden caster sugar
- 115 g/4 oz light muscovado sugar
- 1 egg, beaten
- ½ tsp vanilla extract
- 85 g/3 oz plain flour
- ½ tsp bicarbonate of soda
- ½ tsp baking powder
- pinch of salt
- 115 g/4 oz rolled oats

1 Preheat the oven to 180°C/350°F/ Gas Mark 4, and grease three baking sheets.

2 Place the butter and peanut butter in a bowl and beat together. Beat in the caster sugar and muscovado sugar, then gradually beat in the egg and the vanilla extract.

3 Sift the flour, bicarbonate of soda, baking powder and salt into the mixture, add the oats and stir until just combined.

4 Place spoonfuls of the mixture onto the prepared baking sheets, spaced well apart to allow for spreading. Flatten slightly with a fork.

5 Bake in the preheated oven for 12 minutes, or until lightly browned. Leave to cool on the baking sheets for 2 minutes, then transfer to wire racks to cool completely.

Almond Cookies with a
Cherry on Top

Makes 25

ingredients
- 200 g/7 oz butter, cut into cubes, plus extra for greasing
- 90 g/3¼ oz caster sugar
- ½ tsp almond extract
- 280 g/10 oz self-raising flour
- 25 g/1 oz ground almonds
- 25 glacé cherries (total weight about 125 g/4½ oz)

1 Preheat the oven to 180°C/350°F/ Gas Mark 4. Grease several large baking sheets.

2 Place the butter in a large saucepan and heat gently until melted. Remove from the heat. Add the sugar and almond extract to the pan and stir together. Add the flour and ground almonds and mix to form a smooth dough.

3 Roll small pieces of the dough between your hands into smooth balls to make 25 in total. Place on the baking sheets, spaced well apart, and flatten slightly with your hands, then press a cherry gently into the centre of each cookie. Bake in the preheated oven for 10–15 minutes, or until golden brown.

4 Leave to cool for 2–3 minutes on the baking sheets, then transfer the cookies to a wire rack to cool completely.

Chocolate Chip & Cinnamon Cookies

Makes about 30

ingredients
- 225 g/8 oz butter, softened
- 140 g/5 oz caster sugar
- 1 egg yolk, lightly beaten
- 2 tsp orange extract
- 280 g/10 oz plain flour
- pinch of salt
- 100 g/3½ oz plain chocolate chips

cinnamon coating
- 1½ tbsp caster sugar
- 1½ tbsp ground cinnamon

1 Preheat the oven to 190°C/375°F/Gas Mark 5. Line two baking sheets with baking paper.

2 Put the butter and sugar into a bowl and mix well with a wooden spoon, then beat in the egg yolk and orange extract. Sift together the flour and a pinch of salt into the mixture, add the chocolate chips and stir until thoroughly combined.

3 For the cinnamon coating, mix together the caster sugar and cinnamon in a shallow dish. Scoop out tablespoons of the cookie dough, roll them into balls, then roll them in the cinnamon mixture to coat. Put them on the prepared baking sheets spaced well apart.

4 Bake in the preheated oven for 12–15 minutes. Leave to cool on the baking sheets for 5–10 minutes, then using a palette knife, carefully transfer to wire racks to cool completely.

Frosted Orange Biscuits

Makes about 30

ingredients

- 75 g/2¾ oz butter, softened
- 75 g/2¾ oz caster sugar
- 1 egg
- 1 tbsp milk
- 225 g/8 oz plain flour
- 25 g/1 oz cocoa powder

icing

- 175 g/6 oz icing sugar, sifted
- 3 tbsp orange juice
- a little dark chocolate, melted

1 Preheat the oven to 180°C/350°F/ Gas Mark 4. Line two baking sheets with baking paper.

2 Beat together the butter and sugar until light and fluffy. Beat in the egg and milk until well combined. Sift together the flour and cocoa powder and gradually mix together to form a soft dough. Use your fingers to incorporate the last of the flour and bring the dough together.

3 Roll out the dough on a lightly floured surface until 5 mm/¼ inch thick. Using a 5-cm/2-inch fluted round cutter, cut out as many biscuits as you can. Re-roll the dough trimmings and cut out more biscuits.

4 Place the biscuits on the prepared baking sheets and bake in the preheated oven for 10–12 minutes, or until golden.

5 Leave the biscuits to cool on the baking sheets for a few minutes, then transfer to a wire rack to cool completely.

6 To make the icing, place the icing sugar in the bowl and stir in enough orange juice to form a thin icing that will coat the back of a spoon. Spread the icing over the biscuits and leave to set. Drizzle with melted chocolate. Leave the chocolate to set before serving.

Chocolate Spread & Hazelnut Drops

Makes about 30

ingredients

- 225 g/8 oz butter, softened
- 140 g/5 oz caster sugar
- 1 egg yolk, lightly beaten
- 2 tsp vanilla extract
- 225 g/8 oz plain flour
- 55 g/2 oz cocoa powder
- pinch of salt
- 55 g/2 oz ground hazelnuts
- 55 g/2 oz plain chocolate chips
- 4 tbsp chocolate and hazelnut spread

1 Preheat the oven to 190°C/375°F/Gas Mark 5. Line two baking sheets with baking paper.

2 Put the butter and sugar into a bowl and mix well with a wooden spoon, then beat in the egg yolk and vanilla extract. Sift together the flour, cocoa and a pinch of salt into the mixture, add the ground hazelnuts and chocolate chips and stir until thoroughly combined.

3 Scoop out tablespoons of the mixture and shape into balls with your hands, then put them onto the prepared baking sheets spaced well apart. Use the dampened handle of a wooden spoon to make a hollow in the centre of each cookie.

4 Bake in the preheated oven for 12–15 minutes. Leave to cool on the baking sheets for 5–10 minutes, then using a palette knife, carefully transfer the cookies to wire racks to cool completely. When they are cold fill the hollows in the centre with chocolate and hazelnut spread.

Pecan & Maple Biscuits

Makes 18

ingredients

- 85 g/3 oz pecan nuts
- 115 g/4 oz butter, softened, plus extra for greasing
- 2 tbsp maple syrup
- 85 g/3 oz light muscovado sugar
- 1 large egg yolk, lightly beaten
- 115 g/4 oz self-raising flour

1 Preheat the oven to 190°C/375°F/ Gas Mark 5. Lightly grease two baking sheets. Reserve 18 pecan halves and roughly chop the rest.

2 Place the butter, maple syrup and sugar in a bowl and beat together with a wooden spoon until light and fluffy. Beat in the egg yolk. Sift over the flour and add the chopped pecan nuts. Mix to a stiff dough.

3 Place 18 spoonfuls of the mixture onto the baking sheets, spaced well apart. Top each with a reserved pecan nut, pressing down gently.

4 Bake in the preheated oven for 10–12 minutes until light golden brown. Leave the biscuits on the baking sheets for 10 minutes then transfer to a cooling rack and leave to cool completely.

Banana & Raisin Cookies

Makes about 30

ingredients

- 25 g/1 oz raisins
- 125 ml/4 fl oz orange juice or rum
- 225 g/8 oz butter, softened
- 140 g/5 oz caster sugar
- 1 egg yolk, lightly beaten
- 280 g/10 oz plain flour
- pinch of salt
- 85 g/3 oz dried bananas, finely chopped

1 Place the raisins in a bowl, pour in the orange juice or rum and leave to soak for 30 minutes. Drain the raisins, reserving any remaining liquid.

2 Preheat the oven to 190°C/375°F/ Gas Mark 5. Line two large baking sheets with baking paper. Place the butter and sugar in a large bowl and beat together until light and fluffy, then beat in the egg yolk and 2 teaspoons of the reserved orange juice. Sift together the flour and salt into the mixture, add the raisins and dried bananas and stir until combined.

3 Place tablespoons of the mixture into heaps on the baking sheets, spaced well apart, then flatten them gently.

4 Bake in the preheated oven for 12–15 minutes, or until golden. Leave to cool on the baking sheets for 5–10 minutes, then transfer the cookies to wire racks to cool completely.

Coconut & Cranberry Cookies

Makes about 30

ingredients

- 225 g/8 oz butter, softened
- 140 g/5 oz caster sugar
- 1 egg yolk, lightly beaten
- 2 tsp vanilla extract
- 280 g/10 oz plain flour
- pinch of salt
- 40 g/1½ oz desiccated coconut
- 60 g/2¼ oz dried cranberries

1 Preheat the oven to 190°C/375°F/ Gas Mark 5. Line two baking sheets with baking paper.

2 Put the butter and sugar into a bowl and mix well with a wooden spoon, then beat in the egg yolk and vanilla extract.

3 Sift together the flour and a pinch of salt into the mixture, add the coconut and cranberries and stir until thoroughly combined. Scoop up tablespoons of the dough and place in mounds on the prepared baking sheets spaced well apart.

4 Bake for 12–15 minutes in the preheated oven, until golden brown. Leave to cool on the baking sheets for 5–10 minutes, then using a palette knife, carefully transfer to wire racks to cool completely.

Chunky Apricot & Pecan
Cookies

Makes about 16

ingredients
- 85 g/3 oz butter, plus extra for greasing
- 85 g/3 oz light muscovado sugar
- 1 egg, beaten
- ½ tsp grated nutmeg
- 1 tsp vanilla extract
- 200 g/7 oz self-raising flour
- 175 g/6 oz ready-to-eat dried apricots, roughly chopped
- 85 g/3 oz pecan nuts, roughly chopped

1 Preheat the oven to 200°C/400°F/ Gas Mark 6. Grease two baking sheets.

2 Place the butter, sugar, egg, nutmeg and vanilla extract in a bowl and beat until smooth. Stir in the flour, apricots and pecans, mixing to form a soft dough.

3 Use a tablespoon to place heaps of dough on the baking sheets, pressing with a fork to flatten slightly.

4 Bake the cookies for 12–15 minutes in the preheated oven, or until golden brown. Transfer to a wire rack to cool.

Gingersnaps

Makes 30

ingredients

- 125 g/4½ oz butter, plus extra for greasing
- 350 g/12 oz self-raising flour
- pinch of salt
- 200 g/7 oz caster sugar
- 1 tbsp ground ginger
- 1 tsp bicarbonate of soda
- 75 g/2¾ oz golden syrup
- 1 egg, beaten
- 1 tsp grated orange rind

1 Preheat the oven to 160°C/325°F/ Gas Mark 3, then lightly grease several baking sheets.

2 Sift together the flour, salt, sugar, ginger and bicarbonate of soda into a large mixing bowl.

3 Heat the butter and golden syrup together in a saucepan over a very low heat until the butter has melted. Remove the pan from the heat and leave to cool slightly, then pour the contents onto the dry ingredients.

4 Add the egg and orange rind and mix thoroughly to form a dough. Using your hands, carefully shape the dough into 30 even-sized balls.

5 Place the balls well apart on the prepared baking sheets, then flatten them slightly with your fingers.

6 Bake in the preheated oven for 15–20 minutes, then carefully transfer to a wire rack to cool.

Florentine Biscuits

Makes 18

ingredients
- 115 g/4 oz butter, softened, plus extra for greasing
- 115 g/4 oz caster sugar
- 1 egg, beaten
- 175 g/6 oz plain flour
- ½ tsp bicarbonate of soda
- 25 g/1 oz flaked almonds, lightly crushed
- 55 g/2 oz glacé cherries, chopped
- 55 g/2 oz mixed peel
- 55 g/2 oz sultanas
- 85 g/3 oz dark chocolate, melted

1 Preheat the oven to 190°C/375°F/Gas Mark 5. Lightly grease two baking sheets.

2 Place the butter and sugar in a bowl and beat together until pale and fluffy. Beat in the egg. Sift in the flour and bicarbonate of soda and mix to a soft dough.

3 Mix together the almonds, cherries, mixed peel and sultanas. Stir half into the biscuit dough. Place 18 heaped spoonfuls of the dough onto the baking sheets, spaced well apart. Sprinkle with the rest of the fruit and nut mixture.

4 Bake in the preheated oven for 10–12 minutes until pale golden. Leave the cookies on the baking sheets for 10 minutes then transfer to a wire rack and leave to cool completely.

5 Use a teaspoon to drizzle melted chocolate over each cookie. Leave to set.

Spiced Rum Biscuits

Makes 18

ingredients

- 175 g/6 oz unsalted butter, softened, plus extra for greasing
- 175 g/6 oz dark muscovado sugar
- 225 g/8 oz plain flour
- pinch of salt
- ½ tsp bicarbonate of soda
- 1 tsp ground cinnamon
- ¼ tsp ground coriander
- ½ tsp grated nutmeg
- ¼ tsp ground cloves
- 2 tbsp dark rum

1 Preheat the oven to 180°C/350°F/ Gas Mark 4. Lightly grease two baking sheets.

2 Cream together the butter and sugar and whisk until light and fluffy.

3 Sieve the flour, salt, bicarbonate of soda, cinnamon, coriander, nutmeg and cloves into the creamed mixture. Stir in the dark rum.

4 Place 18 spoonfuls of the dough onto the baking sheets, spaced well apart. Flatten each one slightly with the back of a spoon.

5 Bake in the preheated oven for 10–12 minutes until golden. Leave the biscuits to cool on wire racks before serving.

Oaty Raisin & Hazelnut
Biscuits

Makes about 30

ingredients
- 55 g/2 oz raisins, chopped
- 125 ml/4 fl oz orange juice
- 225 g/8 oz butter, softened
- 140 g/5 oz caster sugar
- 1 egg yolk, lightly beaten
- 2 tsp vanilla extract
- 225 g/8 oz plain flour
- pinch of salt
- 55 g/2 oz rolled oats
- 55 g/2 oz hazelnuts, chopped
- whole hazelnuts, to decorate

1 Preheat the oven to 190°C/375°F/ Gas Mark 5. Line two baking sheets with baking paper. Put the raisins in a bowl, add the orange juice and leave to soak for 10 minutes.

2 Put the butter and sugar into a bowl and mix well with a wooden spoon, then beat in the egg yolk and vanilla extract. Sift the flour and a pinch of salt into the mixture and add the oats and chopped hazelnuts. Drain the raisins, add them to the mixture and stir until thoroughly combined.

3 Place spoonfuls of the dough onto the baking sheets, spaced well apart. Flatten slightly and place a whole hazelnut in the centre of each biscuit.

4 Bake for 12–15 minutes in the preheated oven, until golden brown. Leave to cool on the baking sheets for 5–10 minutes, then transfer to wire racks to cool completely.

Crunchy Muesli Cookies

Makes 24

ingredients

- 115 g/4 oz unsalted butter, softened, plus extra for greasing
- 85 g/3 oz demerara sugar
- 1 tbsp clear honey
- 115 g/4 oz self-raising flour
- pinch of salt
- 60 g/2¼ oz ready-to-eat dried apricots, chopped
- 50 g/1¾ oz dried figs, chopped
- 115 g/4 oz porridge oats
- 1 tsp milk (optional)
- 40 g/1½ oz sultanas or cranberries
- 40 g/1½ oz walnut halves, chopped

1 Preheat the oven to 160°C/325°F/ Gas Mark 3. Grease two large baking sheets. Place the butter, sugar and honey in a saucepan and heat over a low heat until melted. Mix to combine.

2 Sift together the flour and salt into a large bowl and stir in the apricots, figs and oats. Pour in the butter and sugar mixture and mix to form a dough. If it is too stiff, add a little milk.

3 Divide the dough into 24 pieces and roll each piece into a ball. Place 12 balls on each baking sheet and press flat to a diameter of 6 cm/2½ inches. Mix the sultanas and walnuts together and press into the cookies.

4 Bake in the preheated oven for 15 minutes, swapping the sheets halfway through. Leave to cool on the baking sheets.

Lemon Chocolate
Pinwheels

Makes 40

ingredients

- 175 g/6 oz butter, softened, plus extra for greasing
- 250 g/9 oz caster sugar
- 1 egg, beaten
- 350 g/12 oz plain flour, plus extra for dusting
- 25 g/1 oz plain chocolate, broken into pieces
- grated rind of 1 lemon

1 Grease and flour several baking sheets.

2 In a large mixing bowl, cream together the butter and sugar until light and fluffy. Gradually add the beaten egg to the creamed mixture, beating well after each addition.

3 Sift the flour into the creamed mixture and mix thoroughly until a soft dough forms. Transfer half of the dough to another bowl. Put the chocolate in a heatproof bowl set over a saucepan of gently simmering water until melted. Cool slightly. Beat into one half of the dough.

4 Stir the grated lemon rind into the other half of the dough. On a lightly floured work surface, roll out the doughs to form two rectangles to a thickness of 1 cm/5 mm.

5 Lay the lemon dough on top of the chocolate dough. Roll up tightly, using a sheet of baking paper to guide you. Chill the dough for 1 hour.

6 Preheat the oven to 190°C/375°F/ Gas Mark 5. Cut the roll into 40 slices, place on the baking sheets and bake in the preheated oven for 10–12 minutes, or until lightly golden. Transfer to a wire rack and leave to cool completely before serving.

Chocolate & Orange
Sandwich Biscuits

Makes about 15

ingredients
- 225 g/8 oz butter, softened
- 140 g/5 oz caster sugar
- 2 tsp finely grated orange rind
- 1 egg yolk, lightly beaten
- 2 tsp vanilla extract
- 250 g/9 oz plain flour
- 25 g/1 oz cocoa powder
- pinch of salt
- 100 g/3½ oz plain chocolate, finely chopped

chocolate filling
- 125 ml/4 fl oz double cream
- 200 g/7 oz white chocolate, broken into pieces
- 1 tsp orange extract

1 Preheat the oven to 190°C/375°F/ Gas Mark 5. Line two baking sheets with baking paper.

2 Put the butter, sugar and orange rind into a bowl and mix well with a wooden spoon, then beat in the egg yolk and vanilla extract. Sift the flour, cocoa powder and a pinch of salt into the mixture, add the chopped chocolate and stir until thoroughly combined.

3 Scoop up tablespoons of the dough, roll into balls and place on the prepared baking sheets spaced well apart. Gently flatten and smooth the tops with the back of a spoon.

4 Bake for 10–15 minutes in the preheated oven, until light golden brown. Leave to cool on the baking sheets for 5–10 minutes, then using a palette knife, carefully transfer to wire racks to cool completely.

5 To make the filling, bring the cream to the boil in a small saucepan, then remove the pan from the heat. Stir in the chocolate until the mixture is smooth, then stir in the orange extract. When the mixture is completely cool, use to sandwich the biscuits together in pairs.

Crunchy Nut & Honey
Sandwich Biscuits

Makes about 30

ingredients

- 300 g/10½ oz butter, softened
- 140 g/5 oz caster sugar
- 1 egg yolk, lightly beaten
- 2 tsp vanilla extract
- 280 g/10 oz plain flour
- pinch of salt
- 40 g/1½ oz macadamia nuts, cashew nuts or pine kernels, chopped
- 85 g/3 oz icing sugar
- 85 g/3 oz clover or other set honey

1 Preheat the oven to 190°C/375°F/ Gas Mark 5. Line two baking sheets with baking paper.

2 Put 225 g/8 oz of the butter and the caster sugar into a bowl and mix well with a wooden spoon, then beat in the egg yolk and vanilla extract. Sift the flour and a pinch of salt into the mixture and stir until thoroughly combined.

3 Scoop up tablespoons of the dough and roll into balls. Put half of them on a prepared baking sheet spaced well apart and flatten gently. Spread out the nuts in a shallow dish and dip one side of the remaining dough balls into them, then place on the other baking sheet, nut side uppermost, and flatten gently.

4 Bake for 10–15 minutes in the preheated oven, until light golden brown. Leave to cool on the baking sheets for 5–10 minutes, then using a palette knife, carefully transfer to wire racks to cool completely.

5 Beat the remaining butter with the icing sugar and honey until creamy and thoroughly mixed. Spread the honey mixture over the plain biscuits and top with the nut-coated biscuits.

Chapter 4
Sweet Pies & Pastries

Lemon Meringue Pie

Serves 6

ingredients

pastry
- 150 g/5½ oz plain flour, plus extra for dusting
- 85 g/3 oz butter, cut into small pieces, plus extra for greasing
- 35 g/1¼ oz icing sugar, sifted
- finely grated rind of ½ lemon
- ½ egg yolk, beaten
- 1½ tbsp milk

filling
- 3 tbsp cornflour
- 300 ml/10 fl oz water
- juice and grated rind of 2 lemons
- 175 g/6 oz caster sugar
- 2 eggs, separated

1 To make the pastry, sift the flour into a bowl. Add the butter and cut into the flour, then rub in with your fingertips until the mixture resembles breadcrumbs. Stir in the icing sugar and lemon rind. Stir in the egg yolk and milk and mix to a smooth dough. Shape into a ball, cover and chill for 30 minutes.

2 Preheat the oven to 180°C/350°F/ Gas Mark 4. Grease a 20-cm/8-inch round tart tin with butter. Roll out the pastry on a lightly floured surface to a thickness of 5 mm/¼ inch, then use it to line the base and the sides of the tin. Prick all over with a fork, line with baking paper and fill with baking beans. Bake in the preheated oven for 15 minutes. Remove the pastry case from the oven and take out the baking paper and beans. Reduce the oven temperature to 150°C/300°F/Gas Mark 2.

3 For the filling, mix the cornflour with a little of the water to form a paste. Put the remaining water in a saucepan. Stir in the lemon juice and rind and cornflour paste. Bring to the boil, stirring. Cook for 2 minutes. Cool a little. Stir in 5 tablespoons of the caster sugar and the egg yolks, and pour into the pastry case.

4 Whisk the egg whites in a clean, grease-free bowl until stiff. Gradually whisk in the remaining caster sugar and spread over the pie. Bake for a further 40 minutes. Remove from the oven, cool and serve.

Apple Pie

Serves 6–8

ingredients

pastry
- 175 g/6 oz plain flour
- pinch of salt
- 85 g/3 oz butter or margarine, cut into small pieces
- 85 g/3 oz lard or white vegetable fat, cut into small pieces
- about 1–2 tbsp water
- beaten egg or milk, for glazing

filling
- 750 g–1 kg/1 lb 10 oz–2 lb 4 oz cooking apples, peeled, cored and sliced
- 125 g/4½ oz soft light brown or caster sugar, plus extra for sprinkling
- ½–1 tsp ground cinnamon, mixed spice or ground ginger
- about 1–2 tbsp water

1 To make the pastry, sift the flour and salt into a mixing bowl. Add the butter and lard, and rub in with your fingertips until the mixture resembles fine breadcrumbs. Add enough cold water to mix to a firm dough. Wrap in clingfilm and chill in the refrigerator for 30 minutes.

2 Preheat the oven to 220°C/425°F/ Gas Mark 7. Roll out almost two thirds of the pastry thinly and use to line a deep 23-cm/9-inch pie plate.

3 For the filling, mix the apples with the sugar and spices, and pack into the pastry case – the filling can come up above the rim. Add the water, if needed, particularly if the apples are not very juicy.

4 Roll out the remaining pastry to form a lid. Dampen the edges of the pie rim with water and position the lid, pressing the edges firmly together. Trim and crimp the edges.

5 Use the pastry trimmings to cut out leaves or other shapes to decorate the top of the pie. Dampen and attach. Glaze the top of the pie with beaten egg or milk, make one or two slits in the top and place the pie plate on a baking sheet.

6 Bake in the preheated oven for 20 minutes, then reduce the temperature to 180°C/350°F/Gas Mark 4 and bake for a further 30 minutes, or until the pastry is a light golden brown. Serve hot or cold, sprinkled with sugar.

Sweet Pumpkin Pie

Serves 4

ingredients

filling
- 1.8 kg/4 lb pumpkin
- 400 g/14 oz canned condensed milk
- 2 eggs
- 1 tsp salt
- ½ tsp vanilla extract
- 1 tbsp demerara sugar

pastry
- 140 g/5 oz plain flour, plus extra for dusting
- ¼ tsp baking powder
- 1½ tsp ground cinnamon
- ¾ tsp grated nutmeg
- ¾ tsp ground cloves
- 50 g/1¾ oz caster sugar
- 55 g/2 oz cold unsalted butter, plus extra for greasing
- 1 egg

topping
- 2 tbsp plain flour
- 4 tbsp demerara sugar
- 1 tbsp ground cinnamon
- 25 g/1 oz cold unsalted butter, diced
- 85 g/3 oz shelled pecans, chopped
- 70 g/2½ oz shelled walnuts, chopped

1 Preheat the oven to 190°/375°F/ Gas Mark 5. Quarter the pumpkin, and remove the seeds, stems and stringy insides. Place the pumpkin quarters cut side down, in a roasting tin and cover with foil. Bake in the oven for 1½ hours, then remove and allow to cool. Scoop out the flesh and purée in a food processor. Drain any excess liquid, cover with clingfilm and chill until ready to use.

2 To make the pastry, grease a 23-cm/ 9-inch round pie plate with butter. Sift the flour and baking powder in a bowl. Stir in the spices and caster sugar. Rub in the butter until the mixture resembles breadcrumbs, then make a well in the centre. Beat the egg and pour in. Mix together with a spoon, then use your hands to shape the dough into a ball.

3 Place the dough on a clean work surface lightly dusted with flour, and roll out to a round large enough to line the pie dish. Use it to line the dish, then trim the edge. Cover the dish with clingfilm and chill in the refrigerator for 30 minutes.

4 Preheat the oven to 220°C/425°F/ Gas Mark 7. To make the filling, place the pumpkin purée in a large bowl, then stir in the condensed milk and the eggs. Add the salt, then stir in the vanilla extract and demerara sugar. Pour into the pastry case and bake in the preheated oven for 15 minutes.

5 Meanwhile, make the topping. Combine the flour, sugar and cinnamon in a bowl, rub in the butter until crumbly, then stir in the nuts. Remove the pie from the oven and reduce the temperature to 180°C/350°F/ Gas Mark 4. Sprinkle the topping over the pie, then bake for a further 35 minutes. Remove from the oven and serve hot or cold.

Mississippi Mud Pie

Serves 12–14

ingredients

crumb crust
- 140 g/5 oz digestive biscuits
- 85 g/3 oz pecans, finely chopped
- 1 tbsp light brown sugar
- ½ tsp ground cinnamon
- 85 g/3 oz butter, melted

filling
- 225 g/8 oz butter or margarine, plus extra for greasing
- 175 g/6 oz plain dark chocolate, chopped
- 125 ml/4 fl oz golden syrup
- 4 large eggs, beaten
- 85 g/3 oz pecans, finely chopped

1 Preheat the oven to 180°C/350°F/ Gas Mark 4. Lightly grease a 23-cm/ 9-inch springform or loose-based cake tin.

2 To make the crumb crust, put the digestive biscuits, pecans, sugar and cinnamon into a food processor and process until fine crumbs form – do not overprocess to a powder. Add the melted butter and process again until moistened.

3 Tip the crumb mixture into the cake tin and press over the base and about 4 cm/1½ inches up the side of the tin. Cover the tin and chill while making the filling.

4 To make the filling, put the butter, chocolate and golden syrup into a saucepan over a low heat and stir until melted and blended. Leave to cool, then beat in the eggs and pecans.

5 Pour the filling into the chilled crumb crust and smooth the surface. Bake in the preheated oven for 30 minutes, or until just set but still soft in the centre. Leave to cool on a wire rack. Serve at room temperature or chilled.

Latticed Cherry Pie

Serves 8

ingredients

pastry

- 140 g/5 oz plain flour, plus extra for dusting
- ¼ tsp baking powder
- ½ tsp mixed spice
- ½ tsp salt
- 50 g/1¾ oz caster sugar
- 55 g/2 oz cold unsalted butter, diced, plus extra for greasing
- 1 beaten egg, plus extra for glazing
- water, for sealing

filling

- 900 g/2 lb stoned fresh cherries, or canned cherries, drained
- 150 g/5½ oz caster sugar
- ½ tsp almond extract
- 2 tsp cherry brandy
- ¼ tsp mixed spice
- 2 tbsp cornflour
- 2 tbsp water
- 25 g/1 oz unsalted butter

- freshly whipped cream or ice cream, to serve

1 To make the pastry, sift the flour with the baking powder into a large bowl. Stir in the mixed spice, salt and sugar. Using your fingertips, rub in the butter until the mixture resembles fine breadcrumbs, then make a well in the centre. Pour the beaten egg into the well. Mix with a wooden spoon, then shape the mixture into a dough. Cut the dough in half, and use your hands to roll each half into a ball. Wrap the dough and chill in the refrigerator for 30 minutes.

2 Preheat the oven to 220°C/425°F/Gas Mark 7. Grease a 23-cm/9-inch round pie plate with butter. Roll out the doughs into 2 rounds, each 30 cm/12 inches in diameter. Use one to line the pie dish. Trim the edges, leaving an overhang of 1 cm/½ inch.

3 To make the filling, put half the cherries and the sugar in a saucepan. Bring to a simmer and stir in the almond extract, brandy and mixed spice. In a separate bowl, mix the cornflour and water to form a paste. Remove the saucepan from the heat, stir in the paste, then return to the heat, until the mixture boils and thickens. Stir in the remaining cherries, pour into the pastry case, then dot with butter.

4 Cut the remaining pastry into strips 1 cm/½ inch wide. Lay the strips on top of the filling, crisscrossing to form a lattice. Trim the ends and seal the edges with water. Use your fingers to crimp around the rim, then glaze the top with the beaten egg. Cover with kitchen foil, then bake for 30 minutes in the preheated oven. Remove from the oven, discard the foil, then return to the oven for a further 15 minutes, or until golden. Serve warm with cream or ice cream.

Pecan Pie

Serves 8

ingredients

pastry
- 200 g/7 oz plain flour, plus extra for dusting
- 115 g/4 oz unsalted butter
- 2 tbsp caster sugar
- a little cold water

filling
- 70 g/2½ oz unsalted butter
- 100 g/3½ oz light muscovado sugar
- 140 g/5 oz golden syrup
- 2 large eggs, beaten
- 1 tsp vanilla extract
- 115 g/4 oz pecan nuts

1 For the pastry, place the flour in a bowl and rub in the butter with your fingertips until it resembles fine breadcrumbs. Stir in the caster sugar and add enough cold water to mix to a firm dough. Wrap in clingfilm and chill for 15 minutes, until firm enough to roll out.

2 Preheat the oven to 200°C/400°F/ Gas Mark 6. Roll out the pastry on a lightly floured surface and use to line a 23-cm/9-inch loose-based round tart tin. Prick the base with a fork. Chill for 15 minutes.

3 Place the tart tin on a baking sheet, line with a sheet of baking paper and fill with baking beans. Bake blind in the preheated oven for 10 minutes. Remove the baking beans and paper and bake for a further 5 minutes. Reduce the oven temperature to 180°C/350°F/Gas Mark 4.

4 For the filling, place the butter, muscovado sugar and golden syrup in a saucepan and heat gently until melted. Remove from the heat and quickly beat in the eggs and vanilla extract.

5 Roughly chop the pecans and stir into the mixture. Pour into the pastry case and bake for 35–40 minutes in the preheated oven, until the filling is just set. Serve warm or cold.

Cranberry & Almond Tart

Serves 8–10

ingredients

pastry
- 150 g/5½ oz plain flour, plus extra for dusting
- 125 g/4½ oz caster sugar
- 125 g/4½ oz butter, cut into small pieces
- 1 tbsp water

filling
- 200 g/7 oz unsalted butter
- 200 g/7 oz caster sugar
- 1 egg
- 2 egg yolks
- 40 g/1½ oz plain flour, sieved
- 175 g/6 oz ground almonds
- 4 tbsp double cream
- 410 g/14½ oz canned apricot halves, drained
- 125 g/4½ oz fresh cranberries

1 To make the pastry, place the flour and sugar in a bowl and rub in the butter with your fingers. Add the water and work the mixture together until a soft dough has formed. Wrap and leave to chill for 30 minutes.

2 On a lightly floured surface, roll out the dough and line a 24-cm/9½-inch loose-bottomed flan tin. Prick the pastry with a fork and leave to chill for 30 minutes.

3 Preheat the oven to 190°C/375°F/Gas Mark 5. Line the pastry case with foil and fill with baking beans. Bake in the oven for 15 minutes. Remove the foil and baking beans and cook for a further 10 minutes.

4 To make the filling, cream together the butter and sugar until light and fluffy. Beat in the egg and egg yolks, then stir in the flour, almonds and cream.

5 Place the apricot halves and cranberries on the bottom of the pastry case and spoon the filling over the top.

6 Bake in the preheated oven for about 1 hour, or until the filling is just set. Leave to cool slightly, then serve warm or cold.

Tarte au Citron

Serves 6

ingredients

pastry
- 200 g/7 oz plain flour,
  plus extra for dusting
- 3 tbsp ground almonds
- 100 g/3½ oz butter, diced,
  plus extra for greasing
- 50 g/1¾ oz icing sugar, sifted,
  plus extra for dusting
- finely grated rind of 1 lemon
- 1 egg yolk, beaten
- 3 tbsp milk

filling
- 4 eggs
- 250 g/9 oz caster sugar
- juice and finely grated rind of
  2 lemons
- 150 ml/5 fl oz double cream

- mascarpone cheese or crème
  fraîche and fresh raspberries,
  to serve

1 To make the pastry, sift the flour into a bowl. Stir in the ground almonds. Add the butter and cut into the flour, then rub in with your fingertips until the mixture resembles breadcrumbs. Stir in the icing sugar and lemon rind. Stir in the egg yolk and milk and mix to a smooth dough. Shape into a ball, cover and chill for 30 minutes.

2 Preheat the oven to 180°C/350°F/Gas Mark 4. Grease a 23-cm/9-inch flan tin with butter. Roll out the pastry on a lightly floured surface to a thickness of 5 mm/¼ inch and use to line the base and sides of the tin. Prick all over with a fork, line with baking paper and half-fill with baking beans. Bake for 15 minutes in the preheated oven.

3 Remove the pastry case from the oven and take out the baking paper and beans. Reduce the oven temperature to 150°C/300°F/Gas Mark 2.

4 To make the filling, crack the eggs into a bowl. Whisk in the sugar, then the lemon juice and rind and cream. Spoon into the pastry case and bake for 45 minutes. Remove from the oven and leave to cool. Serve the tart topped with mascarpone or crème fraîche and fresh raspberries and dust with icing sugar.

Ricotta Tart with Chocolate & Walnut

Serves 6

ingredients

pastry
- 115 g/4 oz caster sugar
- 125 g/4½ oz unsalted butter, softened
- 2 egg yolks
- finely grated rind of 1 lemon
- 250 g/9 oz plain flour

filling
- 125 g/4½ oz plain chocolate, broken into pieces
- 250 g/9 oz ricotta cheese
- 40 g/1½ oz icing sugar, plus extra for dusting
- 2 tbsp dark rum
- 1 tsp vanilla extract
- 100 g/3½ oz walnuts, finely chopped

1 Preheat the oven to 180°C/350°F/ Gas Mark 4. Place the caster sugar, butter, egg yolks and lemon rind in a bowl and beat well to mix evenly.

2 Add the flour and work the mixture with your fingers to make a smooth dough. Wrap the dough in clingfilm and leave to rest at room temperature for about 10 minutes.

3 To make the filling, melt the chocolate in a heatproof bowl set over a pan of hot water. Mix together the ricotta, icing sugar, rum, vanilla extract and walnuts. Stir in the chocolate, mixing evenly.

4 Roll out two thirds of the dough and press into the base and sides of a 23-cm/9-inch loose-based flan tin. Spoon the ricotta mixture into the pastry shell, smoothing level.

5 Roll out the remaining dough, cut into strips and arrange over the tart to form a lattice. Place on a baking sheet and bake in the preheated oven for 35–40 minutes, until firm and golden. Serve the tart warm, dusted with icing sugar.

Coconut Tart

Serves 8

ingredients

pastry
- 1 x 23-cm/9-inch ready-cooked flan case

filling
- 2 eggs
- grated rind and juice of 2 lemons
- 200 g/7 oz golden caster sugar
- 375 ml/13 fl oz double cream
- 250 g/9 oz desiccated coconut

1 Preheat the oven to 180°C/350°F/ Gas Mark 4. To make the filling, put the eggs, lemon rind and sugar in a bowl and beat together for 1 minute.

2 Gently stir in the cream, then the lemon juice and, finally, the coconut.

3 Spread the mixture into the flan case and bake in the preheated oven for 40 minutes, until set and golden. Leave to cool for about 1 hour to firm up. Serve at room temperature.

Pear Tart with Chocolate Sauce

Serves 6

ingredients

pastry
- 100 g/3½ oz plain flour
- 25 g/1 oz ground almonds
- 60 g/2¼ oz block margarine, plus extra for greasing
- about 3 tbsp water

filling
- 50 g/1¾ oz butter
- 50 g/1¾ oz caster sugar
- 2 eggs, beaten
- 100 g/3½ oz ground almonds
- 2 tbsp cocoa powder
- a few drops of almond extract
- 400 g/14 oz canned pear halves in natural juice, drained

chocolate sauce
- 4 tbsp caster sugar
- 3 tbsp golden syrup
- 100 ml/3½ fl oz water
- 175 g/6 oz plain chocolate, broken into pieces
- 25 g/1 oz butter

1 Preheat the oven to 200°C/400°F/ Gas Mark 6. Lightly grease a 20-cm/ 8-inch round tart tin.

2 Sift the flour into a mixing bowl and stir in the ground almonds. Rub in the margarine with your fingertips until the mixture resembles breadcrumbs. Add enough water to mix to a soft dough. Cover, chill in the freezer for 10 minutes, then roll out and use to line the prepared tin. Prick the base with a fork and chill again.

3 To make the filling, beat the butter and sugar until light and fluffy. Beat in the eggs, then fold in the ground almonds, cocoa powder and almond extract. Spread the chocolate mixture in the pastry case. Thinly slice each pear half widthways, flatten slightly, then arrange the pears on top of the chocolate mixture, pressing down lightly. Bake in the preheated oven for 30 minutes, or until the filling has risen. Cool slightly and transfer to a serving plate, if wished.

4 To make the chocolate sauce, place the sugar, golden syrup and water in a saucepan and heat gently, stirring until the sugar dissolves. Boil gently for 1 minute. Remove from the heat, add the chocolate and butter and stir until melted and well combined. Serve with the tart.

Plum Crumble Tart

Serves 8–10

ingredients

pastry
- 175 g/6 oz plain flour
- 1 tbsp cornflour
- ½ tsp baking powder
- 100 g/3½ oz unsalted butter
- 40 g/1½ oz hazelnuts, finely chopped
- 40 g/1½ oz caster sugar
- 2–3 tbsp milk

filling
- 400 g/14 oz ripe red plums
- 1 tbsp cornflour
- 3 tbsp caster sugar
- finely grated rind of 1 small orange

- crème fraîche or Greek-style yogurt, to serve

1 Preheat the oven to 180°C/350°F/ Gas Mark 4 and preheat a baking sheet.

2 Sift the flour, cornflour and baking powder into a large bowl and rub in the butter with your fingertips. Stir in the nuts and sugar with just enough milk to bind together.

3 Remove about a quarter of the mixture, cover and place in the refrigerator. Gently knead together the remaining mixture and press into the base and sides of a 20-cm/8-inch loose-based fluted tart tin.

4 For the filling, halve, stone then quarter the plums and toss with the cornflour, sugar and orange rind. Arrange the plums over the pastry.

5 Remove the reserved dough from the refrigerator and, using your fingertips, crumble over the plums.

6 Place the tart on the baking sheet and bake in the preheated oven for 40–45 minutes, until lightly browned and bubbling. Serve cut into slices with crème fraîche or Greek-style yogurt.

Lemon & Passion Fruit Tart

Serves 8

ingredients

pastry

- 200 g/7 oz plain flour, plus extra for dusting
- pinch of salt
- 115 g/4 oz unsalted butter, chilled and diced
- 25 g/1 oz icing sugar
- 1 egg yolk blended with 2 tbsp ice-cold water

filling

- 4 passion fruits
- juice and finely grated rind of 1 lemon
- 150 ml/5 fl oz double cream
- 4 tbsp crème fraîche
- 85 g/3 oz caster sugar
- 2 eggs
- 2 egg yolks

to serve

- icing sugar to dust
- seeds and pulp from 1 passion fruit

1 For the pastry, sift the flour and salt into a bowl. Rub in the butter until the mixture resembles fine breadcrumbs. Stir in the icing sugar and blended egg yolk and mix to a dough. Turn onto a floured surface and knead lightly until smooth. Wrap in clingfilm and chill in the refrigerator for 20 minutes.

2 Preheat the oven to 200°C/400°F/ Gas Mark 6 and preheat a baking sheet. Roll out the pastry on a lightly floured surface and use to line a 23-cm/9-in loose-based fluted flan tin. Chill for 20 minutes.

3 Prick the pastry base all over with a fork, line with baking paper and fill with baking beans. Bake on the preheated baking sheet in the oven for 10 minutes. Remove the paper and beans and return the pastry case to the oven for a further 5 minutes until light golden. Reduce the oven temperature to 180°C/350°F/ Gas Mark 4.

4 For the filling, halve the passion fruits and scoop out the seeds and flesh into a fine-meshed sieve over a jug. Reserve the seeds and pulp. Press with the back of a spoon until you have about 75 ml/2½ fl oz juice in the jug.

5 In a large bowl whisk together the passion fruit juice, lemon rind and juice, cream, crème fraîche, sugar, eggs and egg yolks until smooth. Pour into the pastry case.

6 Bake for 30–35 minutes until the filling is just set. Leave to cool completely. Serve the tart sliced, dusted with icing sugar and some passion fruit seeds and pulp.

Pear & Pecan Strudel

Serves 4

ingredients
- 2 ripe pears
- 55 g/2 oz butter
- 55 g/2 oz fresh white breadcrumbs
- 55 g/2 oz shelled pecan nuts, chopped
- 25 g/1 oz light muscovado sugar
- finely grated rind of 1 orange
- 100 g/3½ oz filo pastry, thawed if frozen
- 6 tbsp orange blossom honey
- 2 tbsp orange juice
- sifted icing sugar, for dusting
- Greek-style yogurt, to serve (optional)

1 Preheat the oven to 200°C/400°F/ Gas Mark 6. Peel, core and chop the pears. Melt 1 tablespoon of the butter in a frying pan and gently fry the breadcrumbs until golden. Transfer to a bowl and add the pears, nuts, muscovado sugar and orange rind. Put the remaining butter in a small saucepan and heat until melted.

2 Reserve one sheet of filo pastry, keeping it well wrapped, and brush the remaining filo sheets with a little melted butter. Spoon some of the nut filling onto the first filo sheet, leaving a 2.5-cm/1-inch margin around the edge. Build up the strudel by placing more buttered filo sheets on top of the first, spreading each one with nut filling as you build up the layers. Drizzle the honey and orange juice over the top.

3 Fold the short ends over the filling, then roll up, starting at a long side. Carefully lift onto a baking sheet, with the join facing up. Brush with any remaining melted butter and crumple the reserved sheet of filo pastry around the strudel.

4 Bake for 25 minutes in the preheated oven, or until golden and crisp. Dust with sifted icing sugar and serve warm with Greek-style yogurt, if using.

Tarte Tatin

Serves 6

ingredients

- 200 g/7 oz caster sugar
- 150 g/5½ oz unsalted butter
- 800 g/1 lb 12 oz Cox or Golden Delicious apples
- 350 g/12 oz puff pastry
- vanilla ice cream, to serve

1 Place a 20-cm/8-inch ovenproof frying pan over a low heat and add the sugar. Melt the sugar until it starts to caramelize, but do not let it burn, then add the butter and stir it in to make a light toffee sauce. Remove from the heat.

2 Peel the apples and cut them into eighths vertically. Core the apples and lay them in the pan on top of the toffee sauce, cut side up. They should fill the pan. If there are any large gaps, add a few more apple pieces. Put the pan over a medium heat and cover. Simmer, without stirring, for about 5–10 minutes until the apples have soaked up some of the sauce, then remove from the heat.

3 Preheat the oven to 190°C/375°F/ Gas Mark 5. Roll out the pastry so that it will thickly cover the pan, with extra overhanging the sides. Lay it on top of the apples and tuck the edges down inside between the fruit and the pan until it is sealed. Don't worry about making it look too neat – it will be turned over before serving.

4 Put the pan into the preheated oven and bake for 25–35 minutes, checking to make sure the pastry doesn't burn. The pastry should be puffed and golden. Remove from the oven and leave to rest for 30–60 minutes.

5 To serve, make sure the tart is still a little warm and place a plate on top of the frying pan. Carefully turn it over and lift the pan off. Serve with vanilla ice cream.

Cream Palmiers

Serves 8

ingredients
- 40 g/1½ oz granulated sugar
- 225 g/8 oz puff pastry
- 400 ml/14 fl oz double cream, whipped
- 1 tbsp icing sugar, sifted
- few drops vanilla extract
- 2 tbsp strawberry jam

1 Preheat the oven to 220°C/425°F/ Gas Mark 7. Dust the work surface with half the sugar and roll the pastry out on the sugared work surface to a 25 x 30-cm/ 10 x 12-inch rectangle.

2 Sprinkle the rest of the sugar over the pastry and roll gently over it with the rolling pin. Roll the two short sides of the pastry into the centre until they meet, moisten the edges that meet with a little water and press together gently. Cut across the roll into 16 even-sized slices.

3 Place the slices, cut side down, on a dampened baking tray. Use a rolling pin to flatten each one slightly.

4 Bake in the preheated oven for 15–18 minutes until crisp and golden brown, turning the palmiers over halfway through cooking so that both sides caramelize. Transfer to a wire rack to cool.

5 Whip the cream, icing sugar and vanilla extract together until softly peaking. Sandwich the palmiers together with the jam and whipped cream and serve within 2–3 hours of filling.

Chocolate Parfait
Sandwiches

Serves 4

ingredients

- 3 large egg whites
- 140 g/5 oz caster sugar
- 140 g/5 oz white chocolate, grated
- 400 ml/14 fl oz double cream, whipped
- 350 g/12 oz puff pastry
- 2 tbsp melted chocolate (optional)

1 To make the parfait, beat the egg whites and the sugar together in a heatproof bowl, then set the bowl over a saucepan of gently simmering water. Using an electric hand-held whisk, beat the whites over the heat until you have a light and fluffy meringue. This will take up to 10 minutes. Remove from the heat, add the chocolate and keep whisking to cool. Fold in the double cream.

2 Spoon the parfait into a shallow rectangular freezerproof container and freeze for 5–6 hours.

3 Meanwhile, preheat the oven to 180°C/350°F/Gas Mark 4 and line a baking sheet with baking paper. Roll out the pastry and cut into regular-sized rectangles to accommodate a slice of the parfait. Place the pastry rectangles on the baking sheet and top with another baking sheet, which will keep the pastry flat but crisp. Bake in the preheated oven for 15 minutes, transfer to a wire rack and leave to cool.

4 About 20 minutes before you are ready to serve, remove the parfait from the freezer. When it has softened, cut the parfait into slices and put each slice between two pieces of pastry to make a 'sandwich'. Spoon over the melted chocolate, if desired.

One Roll Fruit Pie

Serves 8

ingredients

pastry
- 175 g/6 oz plain flour, plus extra for dusting
- 100 g/3½ oz butter, diced, plus extra for greasing
- 1 tbsp water
- 1 egg, separated
- crushed sugar cubes, for sprinkling

filling
- 600 g/1 lb 5 oz prepared fruit, such as rhubarb, gooseberries or plums
- 85 g/3 oz soft light brown sugar
- 1 tbsp ground ginger

1 Place the flour in a large bowl, add the butter and rub in with your fingertips until the mixture resembles breadcrumbs. Add the water and mix together to form a soft dough. Cover and leave to chill in the refrigerator for 30 minutes.

2 Preheat the oven to 200°C/400°F/ Gas Mark 6. Grease a large baking tray. Roll out the dough on a lightly floured work surface, to a round 35 cm/14 inches in diameter. Transfer the round to the centre of the prepared baking tray and brush with the egg yolk.

3 To make the filling, mix the fruit with the sugar and ground ginger and pile it into the centre of the pastry. Turn in the edges of the pastry all the way around. Brush the surface of the pastry with the egg white and sprinkle with the crushed sugar cubes.

4 Bake in the preheated oven for 35 minutes, or until golden brown. Transfer to a serving plate and serve warm.

SWEET PIES & PASTRIES 183

New York Cheesecake

Serves 10

ingredients

- 100 g/3½ oz butter, plus extra for greasing
- 150 g/5½ oz digestive biscuits, finely crushed
- 1 tbsp granulated sugar
- 900 g/2 lb cream cheese
- 250 g/9 oz caster sugar
- 2 tbsp plain flour
- 1 tsp vanilla extract
- finely grated zest of 1 orange
- finely grated zest of 1 lemon
- 3 eggs
- 2 egg yolks
- 300 ml/10 fl oz double cream

1 Preheat the oven to 180°C/350°F/ Gas Mark 4. Place a small saucepan over a low heat, add the butter and heat until it melts, then remove from the heat, stir in the crushed biscuits and granulated sugar and mix thoroughly. Press the biscuit mixture tightly into the base of a 23-cm/9-inch springform cake tin. Place in the preheated oven and bake for 10 minutes. Remove from the oven and leave to cool on a wire rack.

2 Increase the oven temperature to 200°C/400°F/Gas Mark 6. In a food processor, blend the cheese until creamy, then gradually add the caster sugar and flour and beat until smooth. Increase the speed and beat in the vanilla extract, orange zest and lemon zest, then beat in the eggs and egg yolks one at a time. Finally, beat in the cream. Scrape any excess from the sides and paddles of the beater into the mixture. It should be light and fluffy – beat on a faster setting if you need to.

3 Butter the sides of the cake tin and pour in the filling. Smooth the top, transfer to the preheated oven and bake for 15 minutes, then reduce the temperature to 110°C/225°F/Gas Mark ¼ and bake for a further 30 minutes. Turn off the oven and leave the cheesecake in it for 2 hours to cool and set. Cover and refrigerate overnight.

4 Slide a knife around the edge of the cake then unfasten the tin, cut the cheesecake into slices and serve.

Chapter 5
Bread & Savoury

Crusty White Bread

Makes 1 medium loaf

ingredients
- 1 egg
- 1 egg yolk
- lukewarm water, as required
- 500 g/1 lb 2 oz strong white bread flour, plus extra for dusting
- 1½ tsp salt
- 2 tsp sugar
- 1 tsp easy-blend dried yeast
- 25 g/1 oz butter, diced
- sunflower oil, for greasing

1 Place the egg and egg yolk in a jug and beat lightly to mix. Add enough lukewarm water to make up to 300 ml/ 10 fl oz. Stir well.

2 Place the flour, salt, sugar and yeast in a large bowl. Add the butter and rub it in with your fingertips until the mixture resembles breadcrumbs. Make a well in the centre, add the egg mixture and work to a smooth dough.

3 Turn out onto a lightly floured surface and knead well for about 10 minutes, until smooth. Brush a bowl with oil. Shape the dough into a ball, place it in the bowl and put the bowl into a plastic bag or cover with a damp tea towel. Leave to rise in a warm place for 1 hour, until the dough has doubled in volume.

4 Oil a loaf tin. Turn the dough out onto a lightly floured surface and knead for 1 minute until smooth. Shape the dough the length of the tin and three times the width. Fold the dough into three lengthways and place it in the tin with the join underneath. Cover and leave in a warm place for 30 minutes until it has risen above the tin.

5 Preheat the oven to 220°C/425°F/ Gas Mark 7. Bake the bread in the oven for 30 minutes, or until firm and golden brown. Test that the loaf is cooked by tapping on the base with your knuckles – it should sound hollow. Transfer to a wire rack to cool.

Wholemeal Harvest Bread

Makes 1 small loaf

ingredients
- 225 g/8 oz strong wholemeal bread flour, plus extra for dusting
- 1 tbsp skimmed milk powder
- 1 tsp salt
- 2 tbsp soft brown sugar
- 1 tsp easy-blend dried yeast
- 1½ tbsp sunflower oil, plus extra for greasing
- 175 ml/6 fl oz lukewarm water

1 Place the flour, milk powder, salt, sugar and yeast in a large bowl. Pour in the oil and add the water, then mix well to make a smooth dough.

2 Turn out onto a lightly floured surface and knead well for about 10 minutes, until smooth. Brush a bowl with oil. Shape the dough into a ball, place it in the bowl and put the bowl into a plastic bag or cover with a damp tea towel. Leave to rise in a warm place for 1 hour, until the dough has doubled in volume.

3 Oil a 900-g/2-lb loaf tin. Turn the dough out onto a lightly floured surface and knead for 1 minute until smooth. Shape the dough the length of the tin and three times the width. Fold the dough into three lengthways and place it in the tin with the join underneath. Cover and leave in a warm place for 30 minutes until it has risen above the tin.

4 Preheat the oven to 220°C/425°F/ Gas Mark 7. Bake the bread in the oven for 30 minutes, or until firm and golden brown. Test that the loaf is cooked by tapping on the base with your knuckles – it should sound hollow. Transfer to a wire rack to cool.

Chilli-Coriander Naan

Makes 8

ingredients
- 450 g/1 lb plain flour
- 2 tsp sugar
- 1 tsp salt
- 1 tsp baking powder
- 1 egg
- 250 ml/9 fl oz milk
- 2 tbsp sunflower or olive oil, plus extra for oiling
- 2 fresh red chillies, chopped (seeded if you like)
- 15 g/½ oz coriander leaves
- 2 tbsp butter, melted

1 Sift the flour, sugar, salt and baking powder together into a large bowl. Whisk the egg and milk together and gradually add to the flour, mixing with a wooden spoon, until a dough is formed.

2 Transfer the dough to a work surface, make a well in the centre of the dough and add the oil. Knead for 3 to 4 minutes, until the oil is absorbed by the flour and you have a smooth and pliable dough. Wrap the dough in clingfilm and leave to rest for 1 hour.

3 Divide the dough into 8 equal-sized pieces, form each piece into a ball and flatten into a thick cake. Cover the dough cakes with clingfilm and leave to rest for 10–15 minutes.

4 Preheat the grill on high for 10 minutes. Line the grill pan with foil and brush with oil.

5 The traditional shape of naan is teardrop, but you can make them any shape you wish. To make the traditional shape, roll each flattened cake into a 13-cm/5-inch diameter round and pull the lower end gently. Carefully roll out again, maintaining the teardrop shape, to about 23 cm/9 inches in diameter. Alternatively, roll the flattened cakes out to 23-cm/9-inch rounds.

6 Mix the chillies and coriander together, then divide into 8 equal portions and spread each on the surface of a naan. Press gently so that the mixture sticks to the dough. Transfer a naan to the prepared grill pan and cook 13 cm/5 inches below the heat source for 1 minute, or until slightly puffed and brown patches appear on the surface. Watch carefully, and as soon as brown spots appear on the surface, turn over and cook the other side for 45 to 50 seconds, until lightly browned. Remove from the grill and brush with the melted butter. Wrap in a tea towel while you cook the remaining naans.

Tomato & Rosemary
Focaccia

Makes 1 loaf

ingredients
- 500 g/1 lb 2 oz strong white flour, plus extra for dusting
- 1½ tsp salt
- 1½ tsp easy-blend dried yeast
- 2 tbsp chopped fresh rosemary, plus extra sprigs to garnish
- 6 tbsp extra virgin olive oil, plus extra for brushing
- 300 ml/10 fl oz lukewarm water
- 6 oven-dried or sun-blush tomato halves
- 1 tsp coarse sea salt

1 Sift the flour and salt together into a bowl and stir in the yeast and rosemary. Make a well in the centre, pour in 4 tablespoons of the oil and mix quickly with a wooden spoon. Gradually stir in the lukewarm water but do not overmix. Turn out onto a lightly floured surface and knead for 2 minutes. The dough will be quite wet; do not add more flour.

2 Brush a bowl with oil. Shape the dough into a ball, put it in the bowl and cover with a damp tea towel. Leave to rise in a warm place for 2 hours, until the dough has doubled in volume.

3 Brush a baking sheet with oil. Turn out the dough onto a lightly floured surface and knock back with your fist, then knead for 1 minute. Put the dough on the prepared baking sheet and press out into an even layer. Cover the baking sheet with a damp tea towel. Leave to rise in a warm place for 1 hour.

4 Preheat the oven to 240°C/475°F/Gas Mark 9. Cut the tomato halves in half. Whisk the remaining oil with a little water in a bowl. Dip your fingers into the oil mixture and press them into the dough to make dimples all over the loaf. Sprinkle with the sea salt. Press the tomato quarters into some of the dimples, drizzle with the remaining oil mixture and sprinkle the loaf with the rosemary sprigs.

5 Bake the focaccia in the preheated oven for 20 minutes, until golden brown. Transfer to a wire rack to cool slightly, then serve while still warm.

Herb Focaccia

Makes 1 loaf

ingredients

- 400 g/14 oz strong white flour, plus extra for dusting
- 10 g/¼ oz easy-blend dried yeast
- 1½ tsp salt
- ½ tsp sugar
- 300 ml/10 fl oz warm water
- 3 tbsp extra virgin olive oil, plus extra for greasing
- 4 tbsp finely chopped fresh mixed herbs
- polenta or cornmeal, for sprinkling
- sea salt, for sprinkling

1 Combine the flour, yeast, salt and sugar in a bowl and make a well in the centre. Gradually stir in most of the water and 2 tablespoons of the olive oil to make a dough. Gradually add the remaining water, if necessary, drawing in all the flour.

2 Turn out onto a lightly floured surface and knead. Transfer to a bowl and lightly knead in the herbs for 10 minutes, until soft but not sticky. Wash the bowl and lightly coat with olive oil.

3 Shape the dough into a ball, put it in the bowl and turn the dough over so it is coated. Cover tightly with a tea towel or lightly greased clingfilm and set aside in a warm place to rise until the dough has doubled in volume. Meanwhile, sprinkle polenta over a baking sheet.

4 Turn the dough out onto a lightly floured surface and knead lightly. Cover with the upturned bowl and leave for 10 minutes. Meanwhile, preheat the oven to 230°C/450°F/Gas Mark 8.

5 Roll out and pat the dough into a 25-cm/10-inch circle, about 1 cm/½ inch thick, and carefully transfer it to the prepared baking sheet. Cover the dough with a tea towel and leave to rise again for 15 minutes.

6 Using a lightly oiled finger, poke indentations all over the surface of the loaf. Drizzle over the remaining olive oil and sprinkle lightly with sea salt. Bake in the preheated oven for 15 minutes, or until golden and the loaf sounds hollow when tapped on the bottom. Transfer the loaf to a wire rack to cool completely.

Flatbread with Onion & Rosemary

Makes 1 loaf

ingredients

- 450 g/1 lb strong white bread flour, plus extra for dusting
- ½ tsp salt
- 1½ tsp easy-blend dried yeast
- 2 tbsp chopped fresh rosemary, plus small sprigs to garnish
- 5 tbsp extra virgin olive oil, plus extra for brushing
- 300 ml/10 fl oz lukewarm water
- 1 red onion, thinly sliced and pushed out into rings
- 1 tbsp coarse sea salt

1 Sift the flour and salt together into a bowl and stir in the yeast and rosemary. Make a well in the centre and pour in 3 tablespoons of the olive oil and the lukewarm water. Stir well with a wooden spoon until the dough begins to come together, then knead with your hands until it leaves the side of the bowl. Turn out onto a lightly floured surface and knead well for about 10 minutes, until smooth and elastic.

2 Brush a bowl with oil. Shape the dough into a ball, put it in the bowl and put the bowl into a plastic bag or cover with a damp tea towel. Leave to rise in a warm place for 1 hour, until the dough has doubled in volume.

3 Brush a baking sheet with oil. Turn out the dough onto a lightly floured surface, knock back with your fist and knead for 1 minute. Roll out the dough to a round about 30 cm/12 inches in diameter and put it on the prepared baking sheet. Put the baking sheet into a plastic bag or cover with a damp tea towel and leave to rise in a warm place for 20–30 minutes.

4 Preheat the oven to 200°C/400°F/Gas Mark 6. Using the handle of a wooden spoon, make indentations all over the surface of the loaf. Spread the onion rings over the top, drizzle with the remaining oil and sprinkle with the sea salt. Bake for 20 minutes in the preheated oven. Sprinkle with the rosemary sprigs, return to the oven and bake for a further 5 minutes, until golden brown. Transfer to a wire rack to cool slightly and serve warm.

Irish Soda Bread

Makes 1 loaf

ingredients

- 450 g/1 lb plain flour, plus extra for dusting
- 1 tsp salt
- 1 tsp bicarbonate of soda
- 400 ml/14 fl oz buttermilk

1 Preheat the oven to 220°C/425°F/ Gas Mark 7.

2 Sift the flour, salt and bicarbonate of soda into a mixing bowl. Make a well in the centre of the dry ingredients and pour in most of the buttermilk.

3 Mix well together using your hands. The dough should be very soft but not too wet. If necessary, add the remaining buttermilk.

4 Turn the dough out onto a lightly floured surface and knead it lightly. Shape into a 20-cm/8-inch round.

5 Place the bread on the prepared baking sheet, cut a cross in the top and bake in the preheated oven for 25–30 minutes. Test that the loaf is cooked by tapping on the base with your knuckles – it should sound hollow.

Bagels

Makes 10

ingredients

- 350 g/12 oz strong white bread flour, plus extra for dusting
- 2 tsp salt
- 1 sachet easy-blend dried yeast
- 1 tbsp lightly beaten egg
- 200 ml/7 fl oz lukewarm water
- vegetable oil, for brushing
- 1 egg white
- 2 tsp water
- 2 tbsp caraway seeds

1 Sift the flour and salt together into a bowl and stir in the yeast. Make a well in the centre, pour in the egg and lukewarm water and mix to a dough. Turn out onto a lightly floured surface and knead well for about 10 minutes, until smooth.

2 Brush a bowl with vegetable oil. Shape the dough into a ball, place it in the bowl and put the bowl into a plastic bag or cover with a damp tea towel. Leave to rise in a warm place for 1 hour, until the dough has doubled in volume.

3 Brush two baking sheets with oil and dust a tray with flour. Turn out the dough onto a lightly floured surface and knock back with your fist. Knead for 2 minutes, then divide into 10 pieces. Shape each piece into a ball and leave to rest for 5 minutes. Gently flatten each ball with a lightly floured hand and make a hole in the centre with the handle of a wooden spoon. Put the bagels on the floured tray, put the tray in a plastic bag or cover with a damp tea towel and leave to rise in a warm place for 20 minutes.

4 Meanwhile, preheat the oven to 220°C/425°F/Gas Mark 7 and bring a large pan of water to the boil. Lower the heat until the water is barely simmering, then add two bagels. Poach for 1 minute, then turn over and poach for a further 30 seconds. Remove with a slotted spoon and drain on a tea towel. Poach the remaining bagels in the same way.

5 Transfer the bagels to the prepared baking sheets. Beat the egg white with the water in a bowl and brush it over the bagels. Sprinkle with the caraway seeds and bake in the preheated oven for 25–30 minutes, until golden brown. Transfer to a wire rack to cool.

English Muffins

Makes 10–12 muffins

Ingredients

- 450 g/1 lb strong white bread flour, plus extra for dusting
- ½ tsp salt
- 1 tsp caster sugar
- 1½ tsp easy-blend dried yeast
- 250 ml/9 fl oz lukewarm water
- 125 ml/4 fl oz natural yogurt
- vegetable oil, for brushing
- 40 g/1½ oz semolina

1 Sift the flour and salt together into a bowl and stir in the sugar and yeast. Make a well in the centre and add the lukewarm water and yogurt. Stir with a wooden spoon until the dough begins to come together, then knead with your hands until it comes away from the side of the bowl. Turn out onto a lightly floured surface and knead for 5–10 minutes, until smooth and elastic.

2 Brush a bowl with oil. Shape the dough into a ball, put it in the bowl and put the bowl into a plastic bag or cover with a damp tea towel. Leave to rise in a warm place for 30–40 minutes, until the dough has doubled in volume.

3 Dust a baking sheet with flour. Turn out the dough onto a lightly floured surface and knead lightly. Roll out to a thickness of 2 cm/¾ in. Stamp out 10–12 rounds with a 7.5-cm/3-in biscuit cutter and sprinkle each round with semolina. Transfer the muffins to the prepared baking sheet, put it into a plastic bag or cover with a damp tea towel and leave to rise in a warm place for 30–40 minutes.

4 Heat a griddle or large frying pan over a medium–high heat and brush lightly with oil. Add half the muffins and cook for 7–8 minutes on each side, until golden brown. Cook the remaining muffins in the same way.

5 To serve, split the muffins in half and toast lightly. Alternatively, leave to cool and store in an airtight container for up to 2 days.

Cheese & Chive Bread

Serves 8

ingredients

- 225 g/8 oz self-raising flour
- 1 tsp salt
- 1 tsp mustard powder
- 100 g/3½ oz mature cheese, grated
- 2 tbsp chopped fresh chives
- 1 egg, beaten
- 2 tbsp butter, melted, plus extra for greasing
- 150 ml/5 fl oz milk

1 Preheat the oven to 190°C/375°F/Gas Mark 5. Grease a 23-cm/9-inch square cake tin with a little butter and line the base with baking paper.

2 Sieve the flour, salt and mustard powder into a large mixing bowl. Reserve 3 tablespoons of the grated mature cheese for sprinkling over the top of the loaf before baking in the oven.

3 Stir the remaining grated cheese into the bowl, together with the chopped fresh chives. Mix well together. Add the beaten egg, melted butter and milk to the dry ingredients and stir the mixture thoroughly to combine.

4 Pour the mixture into the prepared tin and spread with a knife. Sprinkle over the reserved grated cheese.

5 Bake in the preheated oven for about 30 minutes. Leave the bread to cool slightly in the tin. Turn out onto a wire rack to cool completely. Cut into triangles to serve.

Olive & Sun-dried Tomato Bread

Makes 2 loaves

ingredients

- 400 g/14 oz plain flour, plus extra for dusting
- 1 tsp salt
- 1 sachet easy-blend dried yeast
- 1 tsp brown sugar
- 1 tbsp chopped fresh thyme
- 200 ml/7 fl oz lukewarm water
- 4 tbsp olive oil, plus extra for brushing
- 55 g/2 oz black olives, stoned and sliced
- 55 g/2 oz green olives, stoned and sliced
- 100 g/3½ oz sun-dried tomatoes in oil, drained and sliced
- 1 egg yolk, beaten

1 Sift the flour and salt together into a bowl and stir in the yeast, sugar and thyme. Make a well in the centre and pour in the lukewarm water and olive oil. Stir well with a wooden spoon until the dough begins to come together, then knead with your hands until it leaves the side of the bowl. Turn out onto a lightly floured surface and knead in the olives and sun-dried tomatoes, then knead for a further 5 minutes, until the dough is smooth and elastic.

2 Brush a bowl with oil. Shape the dough into a ball, put it in the bowl and put the bowl into a plastic bag or cover with a damp tea towel. Leave to rise in a warm place for 1–1½ hours, until the dough has doubled in volume.

3 Dust a baking sheet with flour. Turn out the dough onto a lightly floured surface and knock back with your fist. Cut it in half and with lightly floured hands, shape each half into a round or oval. Put them on the prepared baking sheet and put the baking sheet into a plastic bag or cover with a damp tea towel. Leave to rise in a warm place for 45 minutes.

4 Preheat the oven to 200°C/400°F/Gas Mark 6. Make three shallow diagonal slashes on the top of each loaf and brush with the beaten egg yolk. Bake for 40 minutes in the preheated oven, until golden brown and the loaves sound hollow when tapped on the base with your knuckles. Transfer to a wire rack to cool.

Brioche Plait

Makes 1 loaf

ingredients

- 350 g/12 oz strong plain white flour, plus extra for dusting
- ½ tsp salt
- 115 g/4 oz unsalted butter, chilled and diced, plus extra for greasing
- 25 g/1 oz caster sugar
- 7g sachet easy-blend dried yeast
- 2 eggs, beaten
- 75 ml/2½ fl oz warm milk
- olive oil, for oiling
- beaten egg, to glaze

1 Sift the flour and salt into a large mixing bowl. Add the butter and rub into the flour with your fingertips. Stir in the sugar and dried yeast. Make a well in the centre.

2 Pour the eggs and milk into the bowl. Stir well to make a soft dough. Turn the dough onto a lightly floured surface and knead for 5–10 minutes until the dough is smooth and elastic, sprinkling with a little more flour if the dough becomes sticky.

3 Grease a large baking sheet. Divide the dough into three equal pieces and shape each into a rope about 35 cm/14 inches long. Place the ropes side by side and press them together at one end. Plait the ropes then pinch the ends together.

4 Transfer the plait to the baking tray, cover loosely with oiled cling film and leave in a warm place for about 1 hour or until almost doubled in size.

5 Preheat the oven to 190ºC/375ºF/ Gas Mark 5. Brush the plait with the beaten egg. Bake in the preheated oven for 30–35 minutes until risen and golden brown, covering loosely with foil after 25 minutes to prevent over browning. Serve warm.

Tomato & Basil Muffins

Makes 12

ingredients
- sunflower oil, for greasing
- 280 g/10 oz plain flour
- 1 tbsp baking powder
- pinch of salt
- freshly ground black pepper
- 100 g/3½ oz sun-dried tomatoes in oil, drained (oil reserved) and finely chopped
- 2 eggs
- 250 ml/9 fl oz buttermilk
- 4 tbsp chopped fresh basil leaves
- 1 garlic clove, crushed
- 10 g/¼ oz freshly grated Parmesan cheese

1 Preheat the oven to 200°C/400°F/ Gas Mark 6. Grease a 12-hole muffin tin. Sift together the flour, baking powder, salt and pepper to taste into a large bowl. Stir in the sun-dried tomatoes.

2 Place the eggs in a large jug or bowl and beat lightly, then beat in the buttermilk, 6 tablespoons of the reserved oil from the tomatoes, the basil and garlic. Make a well in the centre of the dry ingredients and pour in the beaten liquid ingredients. Stir gently until just combined; do not overmix. Spoon the mixture into the muffin tin. Scatter the Parmesan cheese over the tops of the muffins.

3 Bake in the preheated oven for 20 minutes, or until well risen, golden brown and firm to the touch. Leave to cool in the tin for 5 minutes then serve warm.

Chilli Cornbread Muffins

Makes 12

ingredients

- 175 g/6 oz plain flour
- 4 tsp baking powder
- 175 g/6 oz cornmeal/polenta
- 2 tbsp caster sugar
- 1 tsp salt
- 4 spring onions, trimmed and finely chopped
- 1 red chilli, deseeded and finely chopped
- 3 eggs, beaten
- 150 ml/5 fl oz natural yogurt
- 150 ml/5 fl oz milk

1 Preheat the oven to 200ºC/400ºF/ Gas Mark 6. Line a 12-hole muffin tin with paper cases.

2 Sift the flour and baking powder into a large bowl. Stir in the cornmeal, sugar, salt, spring onions and chilli. Beat together the eggs, yogurt and milk then pour into the flour mixture and beat until just combined. Spoon the mixture into the muffin cases.

3 Bake the muffins in the preheated oven for 15–20 minutes until risen, golden and just firm to the touch. Serve warm.

Walnut & Pecorino Scones

Makes about 16

ingredients
- 450 g/1 lb self-raising flour, plus extra for dusting
- pinch of salt
- 85 g/3 oz butter, diced, plus extra for greasing
- 50 g/1¾ oz caster sugar
- 50 g/1¾ oz pecorino cheese
- 100 g/3½ oz walnut pieces
- about 300 ml/10 fl oz milk

1 Preheat the oven to 200°C/400°F/ Gas Mark 6. Grease a baking sheet.

2 Sift the flour and salt into a large bowl. Add the butter and rub it in with your fingertips until the mixture resembles fine breadcrumbs. Stir in the sugar, cheese and walnuts. Stir in enough of the milk to bring the mixture together into a soft dough.

3 Gently roll the dough out on a lightly floured work surface until it is about 2.5–3 cm/1–1¼ inch thick. Cut out rounds with a 6-cm/2½-inch round biscuit cutter (make the scones smaller or larger if you prefer). Place the rounds on a baking sheet.

4 Bake in the preheated oven for 15 minutes, or until golden brown and firm to the touch. Transfer to a wire rack to cool.

Cheese & Mustard Scones

Makes 8

ingredients

- 225 g/8 oz self-raising flour, plus extra for dusting
- 1 tsp baking powder
- pinch of salt
- 50 g/1¾ oz butter, cut into pieces, plus extra for greasing
- 125 g/4½ oz mature Cheddar cheese, grated
- 1 tsp mustard powder
- 150 ml/5 fl oz milk, plus extra for brushing
- pepper

1 Preheat the oven to 220°C/425°F/Gas Mark 7. Lightly grease a baking sheet.

2 Sift the flour, baking powder and salt into a large bowl. Add the butter and rub it in with your fingertips until the mixture resembles breadcrumbs. Stir in the cheese, mustard and enough milk to form a soft dough.

3 Knead the dough very lightly on a floured work surface, then flatten it out into a round with the palm of your hand to a thickness of about 2.5 cm/1 inch.

4 Cut the dough into 8 wedges with a knife. Brush each one with a little milk and sprinkle with pepper to taste.

5 Bake in the preheated oven for 10–15 minutes, or until golden brown. Transfer to a wire rack to cool slightly before serving.

Asparagus & Goat's Cheese Tart

Serves 6

ingredients
- 250 g/9 oz shortcrust pastry
- 250 g/9 oz asparagus
- 1 tbsp vegetable oil
- 1 red onion, finely chopped
- 25 g/1 oz hazelnuts, chopped
- 200 g/7 oz goat's cheese
- 2 eggs, beaten
- 4 tbsp single cream
- salt and pepper

1 Preheat the oven to 190°C/375°F/Gas Mark 5. On a lightly floured surface, roll out the pastry and line a 24-cm/9½-inch loose-bottomed quiche/flan tin. Prick the base of the pastry with a fork and chill in the refrigerator for 30 minutes.

2 Line the pastry case with foil and baking beans and bake in the preheated oven for about 15 minutes.

3 Remove the foil and baking beans and cook for a further 15 minutes.

4 Cook the asparagus in boiling water for 2–3 minutes, drain and cut into bite-sized pieces.

5 Heat the oil in a small frying pan and fry the onion over a low heat, stirring occasionally, until soft and lightly golden. Spoon the asparagus, onion and hazelnuts into the prepared pastry case.

6 Beat together the cheese, eggs and cream until smooth or process in a blender until smooth. Season well with salt and pepper, then pour the mixture over the asparagus, onion and hazelnuts.

7 Bake in the preheated oven for 15–20 minutes or until the cheese filling is just set. Serve warm or cold.

Bacon, Onion & Parmesan Tart

Serves 6

ingredients
- 250 g/9 oz shortcrust pastry
- 40 g/1½ oz butter
- 75 g/2¾ oz bacon, chopped
- 700 g/1 lb 9 oz onions, peeled and sliced thinly
- 2 eggs, beaten
- 300 ml/10 fl oz double cream
- 50 g/1¾ oz Parmesan cheese, grated
- 1 tsp dried sage
- salt and pepper

1 Roll out the pastry on a lightly floured work surface and line a 24-cm/9½-inch loose-bottomed quiche/flan tin. Prick the base of the pastry with a fork and leave to chill for 30 minutes.

2 Preheat the oven to 180°C/350°F/Gas Mark 4. Heat the butter in a saucepan, add the chopped bacon and sliced onions and sweat them over a low heat for about 25 minutes, or until tender. If the onion slices start to brown, add 1 tablespoon of water to the saucepan.

3 Add the beaten eggs and double cream to the onion mixture and stir in the cheese, sage and salt and pepper to taste. Spoon the onion mixture into the prepared pastry case.

4 Bake in the preheated oven for 20–30 minutes or until the tart has just set. Leave to cool slightly in the tin, then serve warm or cold.

Potato & Red Onion Pie

Serves 6

ingredients

- 750 g/1 lb 10 oz potatoes, peeled and thinly sliced
- 2 spring onions, finely chopped
- 1 red onion, finely chopped
- 150 ml/5 fl oz double cream
- 500 g/1 lb 2 oz puff pastry
- 2 eggs, beaten
- salt and pepper

1 Preheat the oven to 200°C/400°F/Gas Mark 6. Lightly grease a baking sheet. Bring a saucepan of water to the boil, add the sliced potatoes, bring back to the boil and then simmer for 2–4 minutes. Drain the potato slices and leave to cool. Dry off any excess moisture with kitchen paper.

2 In a bowl, mix together the spring onions, red onion and the cooled potato slices. Stir in 2 tablespoons of the cream and plenty of seasoning.

3 Divide the pastry in half and roll out one piece to a 23-cm/9-inch round. Roll the remaining pastry to a 25-cm/10-inch round.

4 Place the smaller circle on the baking tray and top with the potato mixture, leaving a 2.5-cm/1-inch border. Brush this border with a little of the beaten egg.

5 Top with the larger circle of pastry, seal well and crimp the edges of the pastry. Cut a steam vent in the middle of the pastry. Brush with the beaten egg and bake in the preheated oven for 30 minutes.

6 Mix the remaining beaten egg with the remaining cream and pour into the pie through the steam vent. Return to the oven for 15 minutes, then leave to cool for 30 minutes. Serve warm or cold.

almonds
  almond biscotti 92
  almond cookies with a cherry
    on top 116
  chocolate & almond layer cake 57
  chocolate fudge cake 40
  classic cherry cake 47
  clementine cake 44
  cranberry & almond tart 161
  Florentine biscuits 133
  hazelnut chocolate macaroons 74
  pear tart with chocolate sauce 167
  polenta & almond cake 53
  rockie road brownies 85
  stollen 54
  tarte au citron 162
  vanilla macaroons 73
apples
  apple pie 150
  spiced apple & sultana cake 48
  tart tatin 175
  warm spiced apple pie cupcakes 78
apricots
  chunky apricot & pecan cookies 129
  cranberry & almond tart 161
  crunchy muesli cookies 138
  white chocolate & apricot squares 99
asparagus & goat's cheese tart 216

bacon, onion & Parmesan tart 219
bagels 200
bakeware, greasing and lining 14
baking
  baking terms 31
  top tips 30
baking blind 31
baking powder 13
bananas
  banana & raisin cookies 126
  banana loaf 61
beating 31
bicarbonate of soda 13
biscuits & cookies (essential recipes)
  dropped biscuits 24
  piped biscuits 24
  rolled and moulded 24
  sliced biscuits 24
  wafer-thin biscuits 24
biscuits & cookies
  almond cookies with a cherry
    on top 116
  banana & raisin cookies 126
  chocolate & orange sandwich
    biscuits 142
  chocolate chip & cinnamon
    cookies 119
  chocolate chip cookies 111
  chocolate spread & hazelnut
    drops 123
  chunky apricot & pecan cookies 129
  classic oatmeal cookies 112
  coconut & cranberry cookies 127

crunchy muesli cookies 138
crunchy nut & honey sandwich
  biscuits 145
Florentine biscuits 133
frosted orange biscuits 120
gingersnaps 130
lemon chocolate pinwheels 141
oaty raisin & hazelnut biscuits 137
peanut butter biscuits 115
pecan & maple biscuits 124
spiced rum biscuits 134
black treacle: gingerbread 50
brandy: latticed cherry pie 157
bread machines 29
breads 26–29
  gluten 27
  salt 29
  yeast breads 28
  yeast-free breads 27
  yeasts 26–27
breads & savouries
  asparagus & goat's cheese tart 216
  bacon, onion & Parmesan tart 219
  bagels 200
  brioche plait 207
  cheese & chive bread 203
  cheese & mustard scones 215
  chilli-coriander naan 191
  chilli cornbread muffins 211
  crusty white bread 187
  English muffins 201
  flatbread with onion & rosemary 196
  herb focaccia 195
  Irish soda bread 199
  olive & sun-dried tomato bread 204
  potato & red onion pie 220
  tomato & basil muffins 208
  tomato & rosemary focaccia 192
  walnut & pecorino scones 212
  wholemeal harvest bread 188
brioche plait 207
brownies
  chocolate chip brownies 82
  rockie road brownies 85
butternut squash & orange cake 62

cakes (essential recipes)
  all-in-one cakes 16
  cooling 17
  creamed 16
  curdling 17
  melted 17
  rubbed-in 17
  small 17
  testing (if cooked) 17
  whisked 16
cakes
  banana loaf 61
  butternut squash & orange cake 62
  chocolate & almond layer cake 57
  chocolate fudge cake 40
  classic carrot cake 58

classic cherry cake 47
clementine cake 44
coconut & lime cake 43
double chocolate gateau 66
double chocolate mint sponge 39
gingerbread 50
lemon drizzle cake 65
orange & poppy seed bundt cake 36
polenta & almond cake 53
spiced apple & sultana cake 48
sticky toffee pudding 51
stollen 54
Victoria sponge cake 35
white chocolate coffee gateau 69
see also small cakes & bars
carrots: classic carrot cake 58
cheese
  asparagus & goat's cheese tart 216
  bacon, onion & Parmesan tart 219
  cheese & chive bread 203
  cheese & mustard scones 215
  tomato & basil muffins 208
  walnut & pecorino scones 212
  see also cream cheese
cherries: latticed cherry pie 157
cherries, glacé
  almond cookies with a cherry
    on top 116
  classic cherry cake 47
  Florentine biscuits 133
  rockie road brownies 85
  stollen 54
chillies
  chilli-coriander naan 191
  chilli cornbread muffins 211
chives: cheese & chive bread 203
chocolate
  chocolate & almond layer cake 57
  chocolate caramel shortbread 91
  chocolate chip brownies 82
  chocolate chip & cinnamon
    cookies 119
  chocolate chip cookies 111
  chocolate fudge cake 40
  chocolate & orange sandwich
    biscuits 142
  chocolate parfait sandwiches 179
  chocolate peanut butter squares 96
  chocolate spread & hazelnut
    drops 123
  chocolate whoopie pies 103
  double chocolate gateau 66
  double chocolate mint sponge 39
  double chocolate muffins 77
  Florentine biscuits 133
  frosted orange biscuits 120
  hazelnut chocolate macaroons 74
  lamington cakes 86
  lemon chocolate pinwheels 141
  macadamia nut caramel squares 89
  malted chocolate bars 88
  Mississippi mud pie 154

pear tart with chocolate sauce 167
ricotta tart with chocolate &
   walnut 164
rockie road brownies 85
white chocolate & apricot
   squares 99
white chocolate coffee gateau 69
choux pastry 22
cinnamon
   almond biscotti 92
   apple pie 150
   banana loaf 61
   butternut squash & orange cake 62
   chocolate chip & cinnamon
     cookies 119
   classic carrot cake 58
   Mississippi mud pie 154
   spiced apple & sultana cake 48
   spiced rum biscuits 134
   stollen 54
   sweet pumpkin pie 153
clementine cake 44
cloves
   spiced rum biscuits 134
   sweet pumpkin pie 153
coconut
   classic carrot cake 58
   coconut & cranberry cookies 127
   coconut & lime cake 43
   coconut tart 165
   lamington cakes 86
coffee: white chocolate coffee
   gateau 69
cornmeal/polenta
   chilli cornbread muffins 211
   polenta & almond cake 53
cranberries
   coconut & cranberry cookies 127
   cranberry & almond tart 161
   crunchy muesli cookies 138
cream
   asparagus & goat's cheese tart 216
   chocolate parfait sandwiches 179
   coconut tart 165
   cranberry & almond tart 161
   cream palmiers 176
   double chocolate gateau 66
   lemon & passion fruit tart 166
   New York cheesecake 183
   potato & red onion pie 220
   sticky toffee pudding 51
   tarte au citron 162
   see also crème fraîche;
     soured cream
cream cheese
   butternut squash & orange cake 62
   classic carrot cake 58
   New York cheesecake 183
   ricotta tart with chocolate &
     walnut 164
creaming 31
crème fraîche

lemon & passion fruit tart 171
white chocolate coffee gateau 69
crusty white bread 187
cupcakes
   vanilla frosted cupcakes 81
   warm spiced apple pie cupcakes 78

dates
   date, pistachio & honey slices 107
   sticky toffee pudding 51
dredging 31
dried fruit
   banana & raisin cookies 126
   butternut squash & orange cake 62
   crunchy muesli cookies 138
   Florentine biscuits 133
   spiced apple & sultana cake 48
   sticky toffee pudding 51
   stollen, cakes 54
dusting 31

eggs 13
English muffins 201
equipment 10–11

fats 13
figs: crunchy muesli cookies 138
filo pastry 172
flaky pastry 20–21
flapjacks: nutty flapjacks 95
flatbread with onion & rosemary 196
Florentine biscuits 133
flours 12, 27
focaccia
   herb focaccia 195
   tomato & rosemary focaccia 192
folding in 31

ginger
   apple pie 150
   gingerbread 50
   gingersnaps 130
   one roll fruit pie 180
glazing 31
gluten 27
golden syrup
   chocolate caramel shortbread 91
   chocolate fudge cake 40
   gingerbread 50
   gingersnaps 130
   malted chocolate bars 88
   Mississippi mud pie 154
   nutty flapjacks 95
   pear tart with chocolate sauce 167
   pecan pie 158
gooseberries: one roll fruit pie 180

hazelnuts
   asparagus & goat's cheese tart 216
   chocolate spread & hazelnut
     drops 123
   hazelnut bars 104

hazelnut chocolate macaroons 74
nutty flapjacks 95
oaty raisin & hazelnut biscuits 137
plum crumble tart 168
herb focaccia 195
honey
   crunchy muesli cookies 138
   crunchy nut & honey sandwich
     biscuits 145
   date, pistachio & honey slices 107
   pear & pecan strudel 172
   spiced apple & sultana cake 48
hot water crust pastry 22

ingredients 12–13
Irish soda bread 199

jam
   cream palmiers 176
   Victoria sponge cake 35
   Viennese jam shortcakes 100

kneading 31
knocking back 31

lamington cakes 86
lemons
   classic cherry cake 47
   coconut tart 165
   lemon chocolate pinwheels 141
   lemon drizzle cake 65
   lemon meringue pie 149
   lemon & passion fruit tart 171
   New York cheesecake 183
   tarte au citron 162
limes: coconut & lime cake 43

macadamia nut caramel squares 89
macaroons
   hazelnut chocolate macaroons 74
   vanilla macaroons 73
malted chocolate bars 88
maple syrup: pecan & maple
   biscuits 124
marshmallows: rockie road
   brownies 85
marzipan: stollen 54
Mississippi mud pie 154
mixed peel: Florentine biscuits 133
muffins
   chilli cornbread muffins 211
   double chocolate muffins 77
   English muffins 201
   tomato & basil muffins 208

New York cheesecake 183
nutmeg
   banana loaf 61
   chunky apricot & pecan
     cookies 129
   spiced apple & sultana cake 48
   spiced rum biscuits 134

stollen 54
sweet pumpkin pie 153
nuts
  chocolate peanut butter squares 96
  crunchy nut & honey sandwich
    biscuits 145
  macadamia nut caramel squares 89
  see also almonds; hazelnuts;
    peanuts; pecan nuts; pistachio
    nuts; walnuts

oats
  chocolate peanut butter squares 96
  classic oatmeal cookies 112
  crunchy muesli cookies 138
  nutty flapjacks 95
  oaty raisin & hazelnut biscuits 137
  peanut butter biscuits 115
olive & sun-dried tomato bread 204
onions
  asparagus & goat's cheese tart 216
  bacon, onion & Parmesan tart 219
  flatbread with onion & rosemary 196
  potato & red onion pie 220
oranges
  banana loaf 61
  butternut squash & orange cake 62
  chocolate & orange sandwich
    biscuits 142
  frosted orange biscuits 120
  gingersnaps 130
  New York cheesecake 183
  oaty raisin & hazelnut biscuits 137
  orange & poppy seed bundt cake 36
  pear & pecan strudel 172
  plum crumble tart 168
  polenta & almond cake 53

passion fruit: lemon & passion fruit
  tart 171
pastry
  baking blind 19
  choux pastry 22
  cooking 18
  finishes 23
  flaky pastry 20–21
  glazes 23
  hot water crust pastry 22
  pies, covering 23
  puff pastry 20
  rough puff pastry 21
  shortcrust pastry 18
  suet crust pastry 21
  tips 19
  see also pies & pastries, savoury;
    pies & pastries, sweet
peanuts
  chocolate peanut butter squares 96
  peanut butter biscuits 115
pears
  pear & pecan strudel 172
  pear tart with chocolate sauce 167

pecan nuts
  chunky apricot & pecan cookies 129
  Mississippi mud pie 154
  pear & pecan strudel 172
  pecan & maple biscuits 124
  pecan pie 158
  sweet pumpkin pie 153
pies & pastries, savoury
  asparagus & cheese tart 216
  bacon, onion & Parmesan tart 219
  potato & red onion pie 220
pies & pastries, sweet
  apple pie 150
  chocolate parfait sandwiches 179
  coconut tart 165
  cranberry & almond tart 161
  cream palmiers 176
  latticed cherry pie 157
  lemon meringue pie 149
  lemon & passion fruit tart 171
  Mississippi mud pie 154
  New York cheesecake 183
  one roll fruit pie 180
  pear & pecan strudel 172
  pear tart with chocolate sauce 167
  pecan pie 158
  plum crumble tart 168
  ricotta tart with chocolate &
    walnut 164
  sweet pumpkin pie 153
  tarte au citron 162
  tarte tatin 175
piping 31
pistachio nuts
  chocolate chip brownies 82
  date, pistachio & honey slices 107
plums
  one roll fruit pie 180
  plum crumble tart 168
potato & red onion pie 220
proving 31
puff pastry 20
pumpkin: sweet pumpkin pie 153

rhubarb: one roll fruit pie 180
ricotta tart with chocolate &
  walnut 164
rockie road brownies 85
rosemary
  flatbread with onion & rosemary 196
  tomato & rosemary focaccia 192
rough puff pastry 21
rubbing in 31
rum
  ricotta tart with chocolate &
    walnut 164
  spiced rum biscuits 134

scones
  cheese & mustard scones 215
  walnut & pecorino scones 212

seeds, edible
  bagels 200
  orange & poppy seed bundt cake 36
shortcrust pastry 18
sifting 31
small cakes & bars
  almond biscotti 92
  chocolate caramel shortbread 91
  chocolate chip brownies 82
  chocolate peanut butter squares 96
  chocolate whoopie pies 103
  date, pistachio & honey slices 107
  double chocolate muffins 77
  hazelnut bars 104
  hazelnut chocolate macaroons 74
  lamington cakes 86
  macadamia nut caramel squares 89
  malted chocolate bars 88
  nutty flapjacks 94
  rockie road brownies 85
  vanilla frosted cupcakes 81
  vanilla macaroons 73
  Viennese jam shortcakes 100
  warm spiced apple pie cupcakes 78
  white chocolate & apricot squares 99
soured cream
  double chocolate muffins 77
  lemon drizzle cake 65
sticky toffee pudding 51
stollen 54
  suet crust pastry 21
  sugars 12–13

tarte au citron 162
tarte tatin 175
tomatoes
  olive & sun-dried tomato bread 204
  tomato & basil muffins 208
  tomato & rosemary focaccia 192

vanilla frosted cupcakes 81
vanilla macaroons 73
Victoria sponge cake 35
Viennese jam shortcakes 100

walnuts
  classic carrot cake 58
  crunchy muesli cookies 138
  ricotta tart with chocolate &
    walnut 164
  sweet pumpkin pie 153
  walnut & pecorino scones 212
whipping 31
whisking 31
wholemeal harvest bread 188

yeasts 13, 26–27
  dried 26
  fresh 26
yogurt
  chilli cornbread muffins 211
  English muffins 201